Writing from Sources

A Guide for ESL Students

George Braine
The Chinese University of Hong Kong

Claire May
University of South Alabama

Mayfield Publishing Company
Mountain View, California
London • Toronto

Library of Congress Cataloging-in-Publication Data

Braine, George.
    Writing from sources : a guide for ESL students / George Braine,
Claire May.
        p.   cm.
    Includes index.
    ISBN 1-55934-441-5
    1. English language—Textbooks for foreign speakers.   2. English language—
Rhetoric.   3. Research—Methodology.   4. Report writing.   I. May, Claire Arevalo.
II. Title.
PE1128.B657   1995
808'.042—dc20   95-968
                                                                                                        CIP

Manufactured in the United States of America
10 9 8 7 6 5 4 3 2 1

Mayfield Publishing Company
1280 Villa Street
Mountain View, CA 94041

Sponsoring editor, James Bull; production editor, Julianna Scott Fein; manuscript editor, Margaret Moore; art director, Jeanne M. Schreiber; text and cover designer, Joan Greenfield; art manager, Robin Mouat; illustrator, Joan Carol; manufacturing manager, Randy Hurst. The text was set in 10/12 Caslon Book by Thompson Type and printed on 50# Ecolocote by Malloy Lithographing, Inc.

Illustration Credits

pp. 2, 16, 56, 72, 140: Courtesy of College of San Mateo
pp. 34, 92, 118, 208: Courtesy of William L. Young

This book is printed on acid-free, recycled paper.

To Fawzia Braine, Roy Braine, Gordon May,
Anna Marie Soper, and Daniel May

PREFACE

Writing from Sources is based on the premise that ESL students write best when they are given the opportunity to explore topics that motivate them. In our ESL composition classes, we observe how students draw on their experience of diverse cultures to handle such topics with confidence.

The book is mainly for students enrolled in intensive ESL programs and in sections of freshman composition designated for ESL students. It introduces students to academic writing through a sequenced set of assignments that help them to move from personal, expressive writing to informative and persuasive writing. The use of source material, including summary, paraphrase, quotation, and documentation, is emphasized in the informative and persuasive writing assignments. The book stresses writing as a process and encourages the use of collaborative learning strategies as well as individual activities.

ORGANIZATION OF THE BOOK

Writing from Sources is divided into 10 chapters that form two major sections. The first section, Chapters 1 to 4, provides an overview of academic writing. The focus of these chapters is on the writing process, guiding the reader, and effective sentences. In these chapters, the students review writing principles learned in previous courses. The chapters contain many explanations, examples, and exercises so that students and instructors can select specific areas for emphasis.

The next section, Chapters 5 to 10, is the heart of the book, introducing and developing a portfolio of writing on a chosen research topic. The assignments range from writing based on the student's personal experience and opinions, to informative and persuasive papers that include information obtained from library and other sources. The chapters in this section also discuss methods of development for these papers. Frequent exercises and readings reinforce the concepts taught in these chapters. The final chapter shows students how to apply the writing techniques they have learned in the book to essay examinations.

Finally, a section titled Additional Readings, at the end of the book, provides further examples of the writing emphasized in the chapters. Instructors may assign these readings for class discussion.

SPECIAL FEATURES

Writing from Sources has a number of special features.

- The emphasis is on personal, informative, and persuasive writing. This frees students from strict adherence to rhetorical modes such as example, comparison and contrast, classification, process analysis, cause and effect, and argumentation. At the same time, the book suggests ways for students to use these modes as strategies for development of their papers.

- The link between reading and writing is stressed by the inclusion of readings in almost every chapter. In addition, the book makes provisions for the use of popular magazines such as *Time* and *Newsweek* as supplementary readers. (If you wish to use either of these magazines in your class, you may obtain subscriptions for your students at special student rates. You may call the *Time* Education Programs at 1-800-882-0852 or the *Newsweek* Education Program at 1-800-526-2595 for more information. Some of your students may already be subscribing to these magazines.)

- Students write on a single topic of their choice throughout the course. The topics, such as ethnic and religious conflict, nuclear issues, and the status of women, are thought provoking and of immediate interest to many ESL students. In our experience, such topics generate thoughtful and mature writing. In addition, a single-topic approach allows students to focus their personal analysis and library research; they are thus encouraged to read, think, and write in greater depth than if they wrote on a variety of topics during the course.

- The readings included throughout the book and in Additional Readings are authentic papers written by ESL students. We have observed that ESL students enjoy reading papers authored by their peers, and gain confidence in their own potential as writers of English by seeing the work of students whose backgrounds are similar to their own.

- Summary and paraphrase skills are covered extensively. These skills are essential to ESL students as they move from personal to academic writing.

ACKNOWLEDGMENTS

This book would not have been possible without the support and contribution of many people. We wish to thank all of them, especially our colleagues at the University of South Alabama who used this book in their classes and made valuable suggestions: Jan Joseph, Mary Jane Curry, Brenda Ayres-Ricker, Virginia Rountree, and Bill White; students who used the book and helped in its development by their comments and responses, especially those who permitted us to use their work; William L. Young, for contributing some of the photographs included in the book; Kim Boyles, for helping in the preparation of the manuscript; Jim Bull, Senior Editor, and Julianna Scott Fein, Production Editor, at Mayfield Publishing; and we are grateful for the many valuable suggestions made by reviewers of the manuscript: Ron Balsamo, Santa Rosa Junior College; Karen Batchelor, City College of San Francisco; Deborah Bradford, Roger Williams University; Christine Bunn, City College of San Francisco; Randi Slaughter, City College of San Francisco; and Meritt W. Stark, Jr., Henderson State University.

Finally, we thank our families for their love and support.

CONTENTS

CHAPTER 4
WRITING CLEAR SENTENCES

TO THE STUDENT

This book was inspired by the students in our ESL composition classes. We enjoyed teaching them and reading their papers. We hope you find the papers equally enjoyable and that they inspire you to write with confidence.

The papers are examples of good student writing, although some are better than others and all could be improved in some way. All of these papers began as rough drafts and were revised by the students, often many times, with the help of their classmates, tutors, and instructors. Although we have edited the papers to some extent, they remain the voice of ESL students, expressing their ideas in powerful and often delightful ways.

We have included student papers in most chapters to stress the importance of reading. Writing is closely connected to reading; therefore, we encourage you to read at every opportunity you have in order to become a good writer.

We would like to hear about your experience in using *Writing from Sources*. Please write to us in care of Mayfield Publishing Company.

We wish you much success in using this book on your journey toward academic and professional success.

CHAPTER 1

English Composition and the ESL Student

Over the past decade, the number of ESL students attending colleges and universities in the United States has grown rapidly. There are now more than a million ESL students, nearly half of whom are from other countries. We might say this is a sign that the world is becoming smaller.

The presence of ESL students in American classrooms offers opportunities for everyone. Both American and ESL students can learn about the cultures and ideas of people from other parts of the world. This interaction can foster understanding and appreciation of people with different ethnic backgrounds and languages. Perhaps the greatest opportunity for everyone is a spirit of international understanding and cooperation that can occur when students from many cultures live and study together.

One challenge facing all students, regardless of their language or country of origin, is the need to develop communication skills that will foster understanding among people. The ability to communicate effectively, orally and in writing, is also essential to academic and professional success.

Writing from Sources will introduce you to an important form of communication, the academic writing you will need for your coursework. It will also lay the foundation for the writing you will later do on the job or in your profession. You already know much about writing, all that you've learned in your first language and in previous composition courses you have taken. What you learn now will build on your strengths and add skills to make you an accomplished academic writer.

Before discussing your writing strengths and the challenges of academic writing, let's pause to describe this fascinating language that has brought us together, English.

THE ENGLISH LANGUAGE

In the sixteenth century, during Shakespeare's time, English had only about 3 million speakers. Most lived in England. French, German, Italian, and Spanish languages all had more speakers. Today, about 370 million people speak English as their first language and about 500 million speak it as a second language, with varying degrees of proficiency. Next to Chinese, English is the most widely spoken language in the world. However, English surpasses Chinese as a global language. The majority of the world's newspapers, magazines, and books are written in English. Eighty percent of computer texts and sixty percent of scientific papers are written in English.

English has a rich vocabulary. The latest edition of the *Oxford English Dictionary* lists 615,000 words. With the addition of scientific and technical terms, the actual vocabulary may be around 2 million. In comparison, German has about 185,000 words and French fewer than 100,000.

BOX 1.1	*English Borrowings from Other Languages*
Arabic	cotton, mattress, orange, sugar, algebra
Chinese	typhoon, tofu, chow, ginseng, kowtow
Dutch	brandy, measles, wagon
French	champion, chauffeur, chic
German	poodle, waltz, plunder
Greek	barometer, elastic, magic
Hindi	shampoo, seapoy, bangle, jungle
Italian	balcony, opera, umbrella, balloon, bandit
Japanese	gung-ho, tycoon, geisha, karaoke, kimono
Persian	caravan, paradise, check, mogul, shawl
Portuguese	albino, flamingo, pagoda
Russian	vodka, perestroika, glasnost
Spanish	mosquito, alligator, vanilla, sherry

English has borrowed words from all other languages. In fact, as Richard Lederer says, "English has never rejected a word because of its race, creed, or national origin."[1] Box 1.1 contains examples of borrowings from various languages.

If you watched the 1994 Winter Olympic Games at Lillehammer, Norway, you would have noted the importance of English in the world today. Juan Antonio Samaranch, the president of the International Olympics Committee, did not speak in Norwegian or Spanish, his first language, at the opening and closing ceremonies. Instead, he spoke to the world in English.

YOUR WRITING STRENGTHS

Many ESL students are accomplished writers in their first languages. Research shows that good writing skills often transfer from students' first languages to English. That is, if you write well in your first language, you should be able to write well in English too. In addition, you may have taken English composition courses previously. Therefore, you come to this course with experience and skills that will help you become a better writer in English.

ESL students often have other strengths that will help them succeed in composition courses. They have a wealth of experience because they are

[1]Richard Lederer, *The Miracle of Language* (New York: Pocket Books, 1991) 24–25.

familiar with at least two different cultures, so they may have a broader perspective on many subjects than students who have known only one culture. ESL students also tend to be highly motivated to work hard in their courses and to learn as much as possible from these courses. If you have this experience and motivation, you are well on your way to success in this and other courses.

WHAT ARE THE CHALLENGES?

Learning to write academic papers in English also offers a number of challenges to ESL students. First of all, because English is not your first language, you should continually work to improve your vocabulary, sentence structures, and knowledge of English idioms. In addition, you must learn the principles of composition and academic research that all university students need to know. This text contains suggestions that will help you improve your knowledge of English as well as principles of composition and research.

The concepts of academic writing in English are new to many ESL students. For this reason, you will learn how to meet the expectations of your readers (professors and other students) and ways to incorporate information from library research into your writing.

GAINING CONFIDENCE IN WRITING

Writing creates a certain amount of anxiety for everyone, even the most experienced writers. After all, when we write we express something of ourselves, a part of ourselves that is then open to judgment by others. For ESL students, this natural anxiety may be increased because you may not be totally comfortable in English, which may be a new language to you. With practice and learning, you can overcome this anxiety.

As you study this text and participate in class activities, you will learn many skills to help develop your writing. The most important part of the course, however, will be the actual writing you do, especially when you learn from your mistakes and make every paper an opportunity to improve your writing. The time and effort you commit to your writing will pay off as you gain confidence in this important skill.

ANALYZING YOUR WRITING   **EXERCISE 1.1**

What are your writing strengths? What skills do you need to improve? In a short essay, analyze your writing and discuss your strengths and weak-
(continued)

(continued)

nesses. Think about the comments you have received on your writing from previous instructors. Did the comments specify spelling, punctuation, or a particular grammar problem, such as the use of articles or subject–verb agreement? You may also want to mention particular concerns you have about this course.

Your essay should be one to three paragraphs.

READING AND WRITING

One way to learn English vocabulary and writing conventions is to read in English as much as possible. Through research, we know that reading is often the basis for writing, especially in academic settings. Reading improves our vocabulary and our understanding of how English sentences are put together. We also learn English idioms and other idiosyncrasies of the language. Part of the work for this course, therefore, will be to establish a habit of reading in English, beyond the reading in your textbooks.

EXERCISE 1.2   **EXTRA READING:** *TIME* **OR** *NEWSWEEK*

For this exercise, you are asked to read at least 20 pages a week from *Time* or *Newsweek* magazine. You may select the articles that interest you most.

Weekly Reading Report

At the beginning of each week, please turn in a report of your reading for the previous week. Your reading report will have three parts:

a list of the articles you have read,

a summary of one of these articles, and

a direct quotation from the article, followed by a paraphrase.

Part 1: List of Articles

List the articles you read with a complete bibliographic entry for each article. For example,

```
Willwerth, James. "From Killing Fields to Mean Streets."
        Time 18 Nov. 1991: 103-6.
```

(continued)

(continued)

Notice the format of this citation: author's name (surname, given name), title of the article, name of the magazine, date of the issue, and page numbers of the article. Use this example as a model for the bibliographic entries of the weekly reading reports. If you need additional help in writing citations, see the relevant information in Chapter 7.

Part 2: Article Summary

From the list of articles you have read, select one to summarize. Follow these directions when you write the summary: Summarize the most important ideas in the article in one paragraph written in your own words. The paragraph should contain five to seven sentences. The first sentence should be the topic sentence of the paragraph; this sentence should also mention the author and title of the article.

Here is an example of an article summary:

> "From Killing Fields to Mean Streets" by James Willwerth describes the growth of Cambodian street gangs in Southern California. These teenage gangs may have sprung up because Cambodian teenagers feel a need to defend themselves against other gangs of teenagers, especially Hispanic gangs. These gangs may also result from the breakdown of family life in Cambodian families, especially those families where the parents are suffering from posttraumatic stress disorder resulting from their wartime experiences. Whatever the roots of these Cambodian gangs, they are involved in serious crimes such as extortion and murder. In 1990, for example, teenage Cambodian gangs were responsible for 46 murders in Los Angeles County.

Part 3: Quotation and Paraphrase

Select a passage of one or two sentences (about 15 words total) from your selected article for direct quotation and paraphrase. First, copy the sentences exactly as they appear in the article. Your direct quotation should begin and end with quotation marks. Then rewrite the sentences in your own words; no more than three consecutive words should appear as they are in the original. For both the direct quotation and the paraphrase, include a parenthetical citation that gives the author's last name and the page number where you found the quotation. For example,

Direct Quotation:

"State and local officials have been unable to come up with any comprehensive solution to the gang problem" (Willwerth 106).

(continued)

(continued)

Paraphrase:

Neither state nor local officials have been able to solve the problem of gangs (Willwerth 106).

✓ For further instructions on how to summarize, paraphrase, and quote, go to Chapter 7.

Additional Readings

In addition to the extra readings you use for your weekly reports, you may be assigned other articles to read for class discussion and exercises. Please bring your issue of *Time* or *Newsweek* to class each day.

You will find one student's reading report below.

READING REPORT

Alan Basa

ARTICLES READ

Carlson, Margaret. "Billy the Kid Rides High." *Time* 19 Oct. 1992: 66–68.
Elson, John. "The Millennium of Discovery." *Time* 19 Oct. 1992: 16–26.
Ostling, Richard. "Shedding Blood in Sacred Bowls." *Time* 19 Oct. 1992: 60.
Zoglin, Richard. "Ad Wars." *Time* 19 Oct. 1992: 40–45.

SUMMARY

"Shedding Blood in Sacred Bowls" by Richard Ostling describes the problem of whether laws prohibiting ritual sacrifice violate the Constitution's protection of "free exercise" of religion. Santeria, which literally means saint worship, is an up and coming religion that requires ritual sacrifice. This religion is spreading throughout the country. Animal-rights activists are pressing to have laws prohibiting ritual sacrifices. Santeria followers believe that their ritual sacrifices are no different from commercial slaughtering or hunting of animals for meat. If animal sacrifice is outlawed, Santeria and other religions that require animal sacrifice will be forced to go underground and become far less subject to regulation.

DIRECT QUOTATION AND PARAPHRASE

"Worried about the city's image, irate animal-rights activists, community leaders and politicians united to pass an anti-sacrifice ordinance in 1987" (Ostling 60).

Distressed about the image of the city, angry animal-rights activists, politicians, and community leaders united in 1987 to pass an ordinance against animal sacrifice (Ostling 60).

FIGURE 1.1 *Writing the Old Way*

ORGANIZATION OF THIS BOOK

Writing from Sources builds on the writing skills you have developed in previous courses by progressing from personal, expressive writing to the kind of writing that is more typical of academic work. The book begins with a review of basic composition strategies, including principles of organization. Included in these early chapters are exercises and assignments that will enable you to practice your writing skills. The book next presents a series of assignments in a portfolio to extend your mastery of writing. You will begin with writing based on personal experience and go on to writing based on library research. You will write papers whose main purpose is to inform the readers and papers whose purpose is to persuade your readers to think and act in a certain way.

For both informative and persuasive papers, you will learn how to incorporate information you find in library sources by using direct quotation, paraphrase, and summary. You will also learn how to document your papers so that your readers know where you found your information. In addition, you will learn methods for organizing and developing your ideas so that your papers are complete, coherent, and concise.

As you respond to the writing assignments in the book, you will follow the process approach to writing. Before the process approach became popular, writers would mostly work alone, with a self-evaluation of the first draft mainly to correct mechanical errors such as spelling, grammar, and punctuation. As Figure 1.1 shows, student writers paid little or no attention to their readers and often did not seek help from classmates or teachers.

When writers use the **process approach,** they go through more stages than are shown in Figure 1.1. In addition to thinking about the topic and the purpose of the writing, writers carefully consider their audience (readers). Student writers share their writing with teachers and classmates (peers) and receive comments from these readers. They then review and revise the first draft of the paper according to these comments. Therefore, by the time the final version of a paper is written, it may have been seen by a number of readers and gone through many revisions. Figure 1.2 illustrates this expanded, or process, approach to writing.

Researchers have observed and compared the writing strategies of experienced and inexperienced writers. They have concluded that experienced writers approach writing as a process. Compare the list of strategies in Box 1.2 to your writing strategies. Would you consider yourself to be an inexperienced or experienced writer?

FIGURE 1.2 *The Process Approach to Writing*

The strategies taught in this book, including the process approach to writing, will help you to write papers in your major coursework (academic writing) and later on the job or in your profession. However, the students in general composition classes such as this one have many majors. Therefore, this course is an introduction to academic writing. As you take advanced courses in your major, you may learn other styles and conventions of writing that are more suitable for your discipline. For example, the documentation style taught in this text is that recommended by the Modern Language Association (MLA). Some disciplines, such as business, engineering, and social sciences, may use other documentation styles such as those recommended by the American Psychological Association (APA) or *The Chicago Manual of Style*.

Most of the student papers in this book are not presented in MLA format. The research papers on pages 186 and 195 have been set as examples of MLA format and Chapter 9 (pages 179–181) contains a detailed expla-

---

BOX 1.2	*The Writing Strategies of Inexperienced and Experienced Writers*

This box was adapted from R. E. Burnett, Technical Communication *(Belmont, CA: Wadsworth, 1990).*

	Inexperienced Writers	*Experienced Writers*
Planning	Make few plans before drafting	Plan carefully before drafting
	Do not make notes, etc.	Make notes and lists; freewrite
	Develop plans while writing	Revise plans while writing
Drafting	Concerned mainly with grammar and mechanics	Not much concerned with grammar and mechanics
	Focus on topic and text, not on audience and purpose	Stop often to reread and think of audience and purpose
	Do not reread and reflect on the writing	Reread and think of the organization and content of text
	Write from own point of view, not that of readers	Able to write from readers' viewpoint
Revising/ Editing	Revise mostly at sentence or word level	Revise mostly at paragraph level

nation of it. Be sure to check with your instructor about the format you should use for your assignments.

When you write papers for your major courses, you will often be writing for specialists in your area; thus, a highly technical vocabulary will be appropriate. In this course, however, you will usually be writing for your classmates and your instructor, so you will need to use language and style that are suitable for a general audience.

TOPICS FOR WRITING   EXERCISE 1.3

How have you adapted to the lifestyle and culture of this university? What changes and adjustments did you find most difficult to make?

Write an essay about your experiences or the experiences of other ESL students in the United States. Include descriptive details and examples so that readers will understand the experiences. You may wish to read about listing, freewriting, and clustering in Chapter 2 before writing this paper.

READINGS

The three papers that follow were written by ESL students in response to the assignment in Exercise 1.3. As you read these papers, notice the details and the examples the writers used to make the papers interesting and understandable. Additional study questions appear at the end of each paper.

MY FIRST EXPERIENCES IN THE U.S.

Arkady Bilat

Traveling to a foreign country is always interesting, especially if it's a country completely different from yours. You can delight in tasting new food, seeing new sights, and learning different customs. However, you must be prepared to face some difficulties.

I didn't have a happy arrival in the U.S. As an exchange student, I flew from Moscow to New York in the middle of July. I had no idea where I should go after my arrival at JFK Airport. A man who was supposed to meet me at the airport did not turn up. So I found myself in that huge city without money, travel instructions, and quite alone. It was my first trip abroad and I didn't have any friends in New York. People in the airport paid no attention to me; they were all in a hurry.

After a while, it occurred to me to check the various airlines to see if a ticket had been reserved for me. There were dozens of airlines and I had to go from terminal to terminal, dragging all my luggage because I had no experience in using the special bus that connects the airport terminals. Finally, I found the airline which had my connecting ticket, but my flight had already left.

Then, I thought of making a call to the student exchange program office in Washington, D.C. But, how could I make a phone call without any money? I didn't know anything about collect calls. Thank God a policeman showed me how to do it.

The next lesson was here in Alabama. Once, I was riding on the road when a car began to push me to the curb. The driver may not have seen me. I couldn't stop because of the car behind me. The only escape was to run into the curb. I fell and injured my arm badly, but no driver would stop! I tried to get up but felt dizzy. The cars rushed past. Finally, I managed to raise my arm and a white Ford stopped at once. The driver helped me to stop the bleeding and took me to the emergency room.

When I think back about my experiences, they almost seem funny. However, at that time, I felt unhappy and lonely. I am adjusting quickly to life in the U.S., and each day brings a new adventure.

Study Questions for Arkady Bilat's Paper

1. What personal experiences does Bilat include in his paper? Do these experiences illustrate the main ideas of his paper? If so, what ideas do they illustrate?

2. Are there any places in his paper where you wish he had provided more information? Did he leave you with any unanswered questions?

3. Did you enjoy reading Bilat's paper? If you did enjoy it, what made the paper readable?

4. Can you suggest ways the paper could be improved?

A CHINESE STUDENT VIEWS AMERICA AND MONEY

Qing Cao

Thousands of international students and scholars come to the United States every year. Maybe the typical problem they meet is "culture shock," which means they are very surprised about some of the attitudes that American people usually have.

When I first came here, I thought it strange the way that American people deal with money. China is an ancient country which has the longest history in the world. Chinese people are smart and diligent and know how to save money. Perhaps this is the tradition that has been passed by our ancestors from one generation to another generation.

Some Chinese students here are supported by scholarships, and the others support themselves, even though their relatives can give them financial help. In order to sustain their valid visa status, they must be full time students. At the same time, they have to work to earn money. However, almost everyone does well in both their studies and their jobs. Furthermore, their tuition fees are much higher than the American citizens'. We really have to thank our ancestors for giving us the ability to save money.

But the way the American people deal with money is so different from us. I always remember a story my aunt told me about her husband, Jason, a really nice American guy. He once spent sixty-seven dollars to buy some tools to repair their desk which they bought for five dollars from a yard sale. In Jason's words, it was worth it. He repaired the desk himself. I do not think that any Chinese person would do that. You can buy thirteen different desks for sixty-seven dollars. Maybe American people do not have the habit of saving money. It seems to me that what they are pursuing is enjoying life and having fun.

Another example is my cousin David, an American-born Chinese. He is working as an engineer at Boeing in Seattle. He traveled to Beijing last Christmas season. A few days ago, we talked on the phone, and finally I knew that he had sold his new Toyota Camry to buy the airplane ticket and pay other expenses. Now he has to take the bus to work every day, but he does not worry about the future, because he still has the job and he can still earn money. After hanging up the phone, I wondered whether he would always sell something if he needs money, and then plan to get another new one by working hard.

No doubt every foreign student had this kind of experience when they first came to the United States. The longer we live here, the less we get surprised. Because we know different backgrounds can produce different attitudes, we come to understand that Americans will live in their own peculiar way.

Study Questions for Qing Cao's Paper

1. What is the main idea of Qing's paper? Does she explain and illustrate this idea so that it is clear and convincing?

2. Are there places in her paper where she should have provided more details? Did she answer all of your questions?

3. What did you like about Qing's paper?

COMING TO AMERICA

Sugumaran Narayanan

Harry, in his first week in this country, said that he was fascinated with it and decided to stay here permanently. When Kareem, a student from Pakistan, was asked to comment about the United States after just a month's stay here, he replied that he was so impressed that he would settle here. Moon, on the other hand, was planning to leave just weeks after his arrival because he couldn't eat the hamburgers and the spaghetti served at the dormitory. However, after one quarter in school, to my surprise, Harry indicated that he would like to take the very next flight to Kenya after his graduation. The last time I met Kareem, he was planning to flee the country.

These three are classic examples of "culture shock," the reaction of new arrivals to a culture that is completely different from theirs. The three students above came to the United States with set ideas in their minds. As a result, they end up in shock. Three problems plague international students—apartment leases, sudden increases in tuition and the cost of living, and living among multi-cultural, multi-ethnic Americans.

Poor Harry was a victim of the first problem. He failed to realize that in this country, if one signs a lease, one has to honor it. Harry leased an apartment for six months but left it after two. The owners sued him for recovery of the unpaid rent and for breach of contract. In spite of losing the case and having to pay for everything, he still believes he was in the right. His justification? He says he was a victim of legal and cultural manipulations. In his home country, nobody would have sued him for what he did. In the first place, it is doubtful if a written contract would have been signed.

The second problem is far more widespread. Like Kareem, many international students are ill-prepared for sudden tuition increases. Some schools increase their tuition more than once within a year. As a result, some international students are forced to accept illegal employment. Irresponsible employers pay them less than the minimum wage. The problem does not stop there. The Immigration and Naturalization Service (INS), on discovering the illegal employment, threatens to deport these poor students. To avoid legal action, some students simply flee to their countries. Others, who are more courageous, go to the border and get fresh visas. They return with glowing faces only to realize that another tuition increase has occurred! The vicious cycle repeats.

Mingling with people from different cultures could also be a problem. Being from Malaysia, I did not face this problem because Malaysia is a multi-ethnic nation. Like American students, who are so used to living around people from different backgrounds, I have had the experience of living among different kinds of people. What about students from Japan, Korea, China, Taiwan, Thailand, and some African and South American countries? Most of these nations have a large majority of a single race. Unless they adapt to the multi-ethnic, multi-cultural American society, they cannot survive here. The striking realities of racism and polarization are a shocking new experience for them.

Many schools have come up with ideas and activities to curb the immediate problem of culture shock. Orientations, cultural shows, and international fairs are but a few. Harry, Kareem, and Moon might have had less of a problem if they had attended some or all of these events. They would have found life much easier if they had come here with better information about the United States. My advice is: "Don't rule out anything. Leave all options and possibilities open. Be tolerant, and recognize and appreciate others' tolerance."

Study Questions for Sugumaran Narayanan's Paper

1. Did Narayanan use personal experiences to illustrate his paper? What kinds of examples did he use?

2. What did you like about Narayanan's paper?

3. How is this paper different from the previous papers?

CHAPTER 2

Planning Your Paper

In some ways writing a paper is like building a house. Imagine that you wish to build a house. First, you think about the kind of house you want to build and start planning its appearance, its rooms, and its size. As you plan, you think not only about how *you* want the house to be but also about the wishes and needs of your family. Then, once your plans are complete, you build the house a step at a time. You start by preparing the land and then laying the foundation. From there you build the walls and the roof, and along the way you add windows, doors, plumbing, and electrical wiring. Finally, you add the finishing touches that make the house a pleasure to live in, like paint, fixtures, and beautiful floors.

And how, you may ask, is writing a paper like building a house? The answer is that both are done a step at a time. Writing a paper, like building a house, is a process. In fact, writing a paper is much easier than building a house, because when you write you can go back and change plans, add, subtract, and rearrange parts, and totally redesign the finished paper from what it was in your original plan. You can easily see the difficulties of making such changes in a house once you have begun to build it. With writing you have much more freedom to create, and thus much more control over the final outcome, than when you build a house.

Since this is a book about writing rather than a house-construction manual, let's think some more about the writing process. In this chapter we look at the steps to plan, research, write, and revise your paper, steps that will help you organize your work and produce a paper that meets your goals. The first section of this chapter covers the first major step in the writing process: planning your paper.

STEP ONE: PLANNING

Selecting a Subject and a Topic

As the plans are the first step to building a house, the first step in writing a paper is to plan what kind of paper you will write. First, you will need to select a subject and then narrow the subject to a topic. At the same time, you will think about the purpose of the paper, who its readers will be, and the research you will do to gather information. As you can see, we can divide this first major step, planning your paper, into several smaller parts.

In this course, you will be given a choice of *subjects* from which you will develop *topics* that interest you most. What is the difference between a subject and a topic? A **subject** is broader, an area of general interest such as computers, nuclear issues, AIDS, world hunger, or ethnic/religious

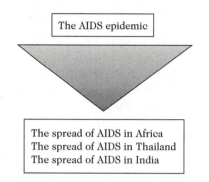

FIGURE 2.1 *Narrowing a Subject into a Topic*

violence. These subjects can be narrowed into **topics** that are closer to your specific interests.

Figure 2.1 shows how we could narrow a subject, the AIDS epidemic, into a topic such as the spread of AIDS in Africa, Thailand, or India. This topic may now be suitable for a student paper. The inverted triangle in the figure suggests moving from a broad subject to a narrower topic.

A subject is too broad and cannot be covered in the few weeks you have to finish an assignment. A topic, because it is narrow, can be researched and written on within a few weeks. In academic courses, you will often be assigned subjects. Ask the course instructor's advice on how to narrow the subject into a topic that interests both you and the instructor. For instance, if the subject is computers, you could narrow it into (1) the use of computers in small businesses, (2) the use of computers in elementary school mathematics classes, or (3) the popularity of electronic mail on campuses. The topic often will depend on your academic major. A business major probably would choose the first topic, and an education major might choose the second topic.

Writers use many techniques to narrow subjects into topics. Three of the most effective techniques are listing, freewriting, and clustering.

Listing

When you **list,** you write down all the ideas that come to your head about the subject. Do this for at least 5 to 10 minutes. Think of the recent newspaper and magazine articles you've read about the subject or the television shows that featured the subject. For example, if you choose "nuclear issues" as your subject, the following ideas may come to mind:

nuclear energy for power generation
pollution-free

nuclear power in developing countries

the North Korean issue

the safety of nuclear power plants

Chernobyl

nuclear waste disposal

inspection of nuclear power plants by the United Nations

nuclear weapons of the former Soviet Union

the *60 Minutes* item on nuclear power plants in India

If you look closely at this list, you will see that some of the ideas are connected—for example, nuclear energy for power generation, the safety of nuclear power plants, and Chernobyl. From these three ideas, you will be able to form a topic such as "How safe are nuclear power plants?" By connecting ideas such as nuclear power in developing countries and inspection of nuclear power plants by the United Nations, you may be able to form a topic such as this one: "Should developing countries be required to undergo nuclear inspections?"

If you choose "gun control" as your subject, you might generate ideas like these:

the popularity of guns in the United States

the high rate of gun-related deaths in the Unites States

the low rate of gun-related deaths in your home country

laws relating to gun ownership in the United States

laws relating to gun ownership in your home country

what U.S. citizens think about gun control

what citizens in your home country think about gun control

the Brady Bill

the National Rifle Association (NRA)

handguns

If you look closely at this list, you will see that some ideas are connected. For example, laws relating to gun ownership in the United States and the high rate of gun-related deaths here may be related. Note also the connection between the low rate of gun deaths in your home country and the laws relating to gun ownership there. From these ideas, you may be able to form a topic comparing the link between gun ownership laws and deaths resulting from guns. Then, after researching your topic, you will be able to compare and contrast the situation in the United States to the situation in your home country.

EXERCISE 2.1   **LISTING**

Choose one of the following subjects. List all the ideas that you can think of. Connect some of these ideas to form a topic.

arriving in the United States	street crime	car insurance
academic counselors	working on campus	roommates
required courses	writing courses	working off campus

Freewriting

Freewriting, another effective technique to narrow a subject into a topic, involves writing whatever comes to mind without worrying about spelling, grammar, punctuation, or complete sentences. You do this for about 10 minutes, without correcting, deleting, or changing anything. At the end of the 10 minutes, you may have a passage from which you could develop a suitable topic. Freewriting can help writers to get started if they hesitate to begin writing.

For example, a student who chose to freewrite on "arriving in the United States" wrote this passage:

> I didn't have a happy arrival. The flight from London was long and crowded. The food was cold and had no taste The plane landed at Baltimore and I wanted to get to Washington DC I didn't understand the accent of the shuttle bus driver and got into the wrong bus I landed at National Airport in DC not in downtown. When I phoned the university, no one answered the phone. So I went out of the airport. A friendly taxi driver spoke to me and said he will take me to the university. He was from Afghanistan and spoke about how much he missed his country when we came to the university, there was nobody because it was Labor day. I had no place to stay and I felt lonely and sad.

This student had an unhappy experience on arriving in the United States. Based on the freewriting, he may be able to develop a topic on the importance of having someone meet a student at the airport when the student first arrives in this country. Although many colleges and universities arrange for this, his university does not.

The following freewriting was done by a student who chose to write on the subject of "computer fees."

> I first used a computer in the Freshman English class. I enjoyed using the computer because it helped me revise the papers but in my electrical en-

gineering courses I use computers mostly for math and design purposes. The problem is that the every time I take a course which use computers I must pay $10. I wish the university would not charge a computer fee for every course. this fee is not fair. Some quarters I have to pay $30 or $40 just for computer fees. My friend at another campus pays only $10 per semester.

What topics can this student develop from the freewriting?

All freewriting will not be as clear as the examples from these two students. However, because freewriting allows you to "think aloud" without worrying about grammar, spelling, and organization, you may be able to generate interesting topics from subjects.

FREEWRITING   **EXERCISE 2.2**

Choose another subject from the list in Exercise 2.1. Freewrite on the subject for 10 minutes. Read your freewrite carefully and develop a suitable topic.

Clustering

Clustering is another effective method you could use to narrow a subject. To **cluster,** write the subject in the middle of a blank sheet of paper and draw a circle around it. Then draw lines away from the subject. At the end of each line, write an idea that comes to your mind and draw a circle around it. Continue to draw lines, write ideas, and draw circles. Later, by clustering ideas that are connected, you may be able to develop a topic.

Figure 2.2 shows how one student clustered a topic from the subject of "AIDS." By clustering ideas like illiteracy, drug use, fatalism, ignorance, and

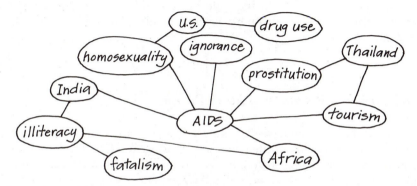

FIGURE 2.2 *Clustering*

tourism, you may be able to narrow the subject of "AIDS" into a topic that interests you.

EXERCISE 2.3   CLUSTERING

Choose a third subject from the list in Exercise 2.1. Then cluster your ideas on the subject to form a topic.

As we mentioned earlier, in most academic courses you will be assigned a subject for your papers and for a few courses you may be asked to find your own topic. For example, here is a list of subjects for term papers from an accounting course:

bartering

accounting for installment sales

accounting for retail land sales

accounting for service industries

oil and gas accounting

accounting for franchises

For this course, your writing assignments will come from a list of subjects provided by your instructor. You may also be assigned a general purpose for each writing assignment, such as to describe your experience, to inform the readers about your topic, or to argue a certain point of view. But you will still have the freedom to create topics according to your own interests, to choose the information you wish to present, and to take a position on your topic that you really believe. You may have to further narrow the topic so that you can cover it adequately within the assigned paper length and time available. You will find help on all of these considerations—narrowing the topic, clarifying purpose, and deciding on point of view—in this book.

Analyzing the Purpose of Your Paper

So far in this chapter, we have discussed subject and topic. Now, let's make a general observation about the purpose of writing. You may think that the purpose of writing a paper is to complete the assignment or to get a good grade. However, these purposes don't tell you what to do in the paper. If you ask yourself the following questions, your true purpose will become clearer.

What do I want to tell the readers?

Why am I writing this?

What do I hope to accomplish?

Who will read this?

Most papers have one of two purposes, or a combination of the two: to inform or to persuade. On campus, you may not do much writing outside the classroom. Occasionally, you may have to write to an admissions counselor, asking that your course credits from another school be transferred. Or you may have to write to the chairperson of a department, to request that a grade given to you in a course be reconsidered. In both of these examples, your purpose is to persuade the admissions counselor or the chairperson to agree to your request.

In writing assignments for academic courses, the purpose may not be that clear. For instance, in an Asian history course, you may be asked to "trace Japan's modernization in the Meiji era." Although the word *describe* is not used, the instructor wants you to describe the gradual modernization of Japan during the Meiji era. The purpose is to inform.

The following assignment from a geology course also requires description.

> Write a brief "commodity profile" of a major metallic or nonmetallic mineral resource. The subject can be one of your choice, exclusive of topics on energy resources. Your paper should cover such areas as the location and geologic character of the major economic deposits in the United States or worldwide, the uses of the commodity, and the production, consumption, and price history of the commodity for the past 10 years. Use figures and tables to present information.

If you read the assignment carefully, you will see that despite the wide range of information that it requires (location, geologic character, major economic deposits, uses, production, consumption, and price history of the chosen mineral resource), you are not asked to take a position or argue a point. Instead, the assignment asks you only to report the information obtained from various sources.

The following assignment from a microbiology course requires both description (writing to inform) and argumentation (writing to persuade).

> Select a research article appropriate to your subject and write a review of the article. The paper should include the following: What was the purpose of the study? How was the study done? What were the results? What conclusions can you draw? If you disagree with the author's conclusions, state why.

In writing the review, you must summarize the article, describing the purpose of the study, method, results, and conclusions. If you disagree with the conclusions, you will have to show why and try to persuade your readers to accept your position.

When you complete your education and begin your career, you will see how these two basic purposes (to inform and to persuade) apply to the writing you do on the job or in your profession. If you are an engineer, for example, you may write to inform management of your progress on a project, or you may write a set of directions telling your staff how to perform some job. You may also write a report for upper management that will persuade them to give you additional funding for research and development. If you are a sales executive, you may write weekly or monthly reports for upper management analyzing sales figures. You may also write memos periodically, explaining the rise or drop in sales and suggesting how sales could be improved.

EXERCISE 2.4   ANALYZING A WRITING ASSIGNMENT

Select one writing assignment from another course you are taking this quarter/semester or have taken in the past. Analyze the assignment to find its purpose or purposes. Bring the assignment and your analysis to class for a discussion.

Analyzing Your Readers

In the analogy presented earlier about planning a house, we mentioned that part of designing a good house is to think about the needs and wishes of the family who will live in the house. A similar analysis is essential to planning a good paper: You need to think about who your readers will be, their needs, interests, attitudes, and expectations.

The first step in analyzing your readers is to know just who those readers are. When you are working in your profession, you will have a variety of readers: colleagues, managers, subordinates, supervisors, and perhaps customers, to give a few examples. For this course, we define the readers as your classmates and the instructor.

Readers' Knowledge

Have you ever tried to read an advanced textbook on a subject that you didn't have the background to understand, such as a senior-level engineering text that you tried to read while you were a freshman? If so, then you know how frustrated you became and how little you learned for your efforts. For any paper to be effective, the writing must be on a level that the readers will understand. The vocabulary should be words with which the readers are already familiar; if not, a good writer will provide necessary definitions. In addition, the writer may have to provide background information on the topic.

For some of the papers you will write for this class, you may be writing about what you have experienced in your home country. Since your class-mates come from many different countries, you may need to describe for them the background information they will need to understand the experi-ence you are writing about. In addition, for some of your papers, you may need to incorporate technical information to make your point clear. When you include technical terms or other information, be sure to provide your readers with the definitions and explanations they will need to understand your writing.

ANALYZING READABILITY   **EXERCISE 2.5**

Compare the following passages written by the same author on the same subject. Passage A is from an introductory book on science. Passage B is from a college-level textbook.

With a partner or in a small group, list the differences in the vocabu-lary in the two passages. Explain why certain words are used in one pas-sage and not in the other. Why is the first passage more readable?

Passage A

Many millions of years ago the world was inhabited by various reptiles which we now call dinosaurs. These dinosaurs were abundant and widely spread; they dominated the land over all of the great continental areas, and they frequently spread to offshore islands. They reigned su-preme through a vast expanse of geologic time. . . .

What is a dinosaur? What are the inherent characters of the fossils that we call dinosaurs? What determines their classification as such? Is it size? Is it age?

The dinosaurs were reptiles, cold-blooded animals related to the crocodiles, lizards, and snakes, and they lived during the Mesozoic era of earth history. Not all dinosaurs were large, as is commonly thought. Many of them were small or of medium size. Taken together, all of them show a tremendous variety of adaptations for different modes of life in different environments. They first appeared in the early part of Mesozoic times, about 200 million years ago, and the last of the dinosaurs became extinct in the Mesozoic Era, about 60 to 70 million years ago.

There are two orders of dinosaurs, known as the Saurischia and Ornithischia. These names are derived from the structure of the pelvis in the two orders of reptiles. In the Saurischia (saw-ISS-kee-ya) the three bones on either side of the pelvis are arranged more or less according to the typical reptilian pattern, making a triradiate or three-pronged struc-ture around the hip joint. In the Ornithischia (orn-ith-ISS-kee-ya) one

(continued)

(continued)

bone, the pubis, has rotated to a position parallel with the ischium, so that the pelvis resembles in a general way the pelvis of birds. . . .

—From Edwin H. Colbert, *Dinosaurs*, 8th ed., Man and Nature Publications, Science Guide No. 70 (New York: American Museum of Natural History, 1960) 4–5.

Passage B

In discussing the life of the Triassic period a brief account was given of some of the first dinosaurs that appeared during the late Triassic times. The early dinosaurs, typified by such genera as *Coelophysis* and *Plateosaurus,* belonged to the dinosaurian order Saurischia, in which the pelvis was a triradiate structure as seen from the side, with the pelvic bone extending down and forward beneath the ilium, and the ischium extending down and backward. In addition to the structure of the pelvis, there were other characteristics diagnostic of the saurischian dinosaurs. In almost all these dinosaurs the teeth either extended around the margins of the jaw, above and below, or were limited to the front portions of the jaws. Most of the carnivorous saurischians retained the general adaptations and pose of their thecodont ancestors, so that they were bipedals, with the body pivoted at the hips and supported on strong birdlike hind legs. Among the herbivorous saurischians, however, there was a secondary return to quadrupedalism. In the saurischians the toes generally bore strong claws.

In the account of Triassic life it was pointed out that the other dinosaurian order, the Ornithischia, also made its appearance in late Triassic times. The genera *Heterodontosaurus* and *Fabrosaurus* from South Africa and *Scutellosaursus* from North America show quite clearly that by this stage of geologic history the basic characters so typical of the Ornithischia were well established.

—From Edwin H. Colbert, *Evolution of the Vertebrates*
(New York: Wiley, 1980) 192–93.

Readers' Interests and Attitudes

One key to a well-written paper is to keep your readers interested in what you are saying. There are many techniques you can use to make your writing interesting, such as the use of descriptive details that help your readers visualize what you are writing about. Later chapters of this book will discuss a variety of ways to make your writing lively and readable. But for now, let's think about reader analysis as a way to make your writing interesting.

What are your hobbies and interests? Let's assume, for the moment, that you are interested in sports, cooking, and international finance. When you pick up a magazine written about these topics, you will usually be interested in reading any well-written article. If you are writing a paper on one of these topics for readers who share your interests, then they too will be interested in reading what you have to say.

Often in academic writing, however, you may not be sure that your readers share your interest in the topic. When this situation occurs, think about ways to make your paper as relevant to your readers as possible. Here's an example. Suppose you are writing about the need for more restrictions on smoking in public places. You may be able to interest all of your classmates in this topic if you provide them with case histories and statistics about the health hazards we all face from passive smoking—smoke that remains in the air after active smokers have lighted cigarettes and exhaled.

When you consider your readers' attitudes toward your topic and your point of view, the analysis becomes even more difficult—but more important. For example, if your classmates and instructor are all nonsmokers, they may readily agree with you that rules restricting smoking in public places are a good idea. On the other hand, some of your classmates may be smokers and therefore resent the many restrictions on smokers that are already in effect. For these readers, you will have to plan your paper very carefully so that they will read your paper without becoming angry. To adjust for the attitudes of these readers, you might plan an unemotional, nonjudgmental presentation of facts and statistics that support your argument for more restrictions on smoking in public places.

Readers' Expectations

One way to ensure a positive response from your readers is to write your paper in a way that will meet their expectations. Since your instructor is one of your primary readers, for example, you will want to carefully follow his or her expectations about length, format, due date, and other details of the assignment.

Research has shown that the papers written in various languages differ from each other and from American academic writing. For example, most writers of Romance languages, such as Spanish, French, and Italian, write beautifully and elaborately. The Chinese, Japanese, and Korean languages are often written at two levels. If the readers are young, the sentences are simple, the writing direct, and the examples specific. If the readers are mature, the writing is indirect, and readers are expected to draw their own conclusions. Languages such as Arabic, Urdu, and Persian are considered poetic languages, and writing is considered a special skill that only a few can master. Especially in Arabic, readers must "read between the lines" to get the meaning. On the other hand, American academic writing is direct and precise, and examples must be used to support the writers' ideas. What is said (meaning) is usually considered more important than how it is said (style).

One of the main purposes of this course is to help you master the conventions of American academic writing so that you can meet the expectations of your readers while you are in school here.

Summary: Planning

The first step in the writing process, then, is careful planning of your paper so that it will achieve the results you wish. A good grade should be only one of these results. You also want your readers to respect your abilities as a writer, and you want to acquire better writing skills needed for your university courses and job or profession.

Allow plenty of time for planning your paper. Choose a topic that interests you and narrow it for the assignment; analyze the purpose of your paper and decide on your point of view; analyze your readers—their knowledge of your subject, as well as their interests and attitudes; and plan to write your paper in a way that will meet your readers' expectations.

EXERCISE 2.6   LEARNING ABOUT WRITING IN YOUR MAJOR

Interview a professor in your academic major (such as your advisor) to find out what kinds of documents are typically written by professionals in the discipline. Who are the typical readers of these documents? Prepare a brief report on this topic that you will present to the class.

STEP TWO: RESEARCH

Research—gathering the information for your paper—is the next step in the writing process. In a college or university setting, you will do the research after you have planned your paper, but before you have begun to write the first draft. However, it may be misleading to label research as only one step in the process of writing your paper, because you may gather information at any stage of your work. You might do some initial reading on your subject before you narrow your topic or decide on your point of view. Later, while writing your paper, you may discover that you need more information than you had originally thought, so you will do additional research. Research, then, is an ongoing part of the writing process.

But what exactly is involved in doing the research for your paper? For many papers, your research will be done in the library, reading books and articles on your subject. Library research is discussed more fully in Chapter 7.

For some papers, you may do other kinds of research. You might interview specialists or authorities on your topic, such as professors or people in your community. Some students may even do field research to gather information for their papers. One student who wrote a paper on problems faced by ESL students at the University of South Alabama used a questionnaire to survey more than 100 ESL students on campus.

LEARNING ABOUT LIBRARY RESOURCES   **EXERCISE 2.7**

Make an appointment with a reference librarian at your college or university to learn what resources are available to help you research your topic. Be sure to check out indexes and catalogs, both printed material and computer services. Write a one-page report to your instructor on what you learned from your library trip.

STEP THREE: DRAFTING

Once you have carefully planned your paper and done at least some of the research, you will be ready to begin drafting your paper: writing the sentences and paragraphs that you will later refine for your final manuscript. It is important to think of your writing at this stage as work-in-progress, rather than a finished product. A draft is where you begin to record your ideas and add information from your research and experience. The draft is *for you,* rather than your ultimate readers; it is far from perfect, but it is a beginning.

Thinking about your draft as work-in-progress should give you a greater sense of freedom about putting your ideas and information down on paper. At this stage of the writing process, you're not concerned with grammar, spelling, or precise vocabulary; you are just writing down ideas that you will later put in final form. It's the content that's important for a draft, not polished writing.

Composing your draft at the computer will help you to record your ideas quickly and will save time later when you revise your draft to produce the final manuscript.

STEP FOUR: REVIEWING AND REVISING

After drafting your paper, or at least a major part of it, you are ready for the next step in the writing process: reviewing your paper to ensure that the paper will meet your goals and receive a favorable response from your readers. When reviewing your paper, you note the places where the paper is weak. You look for ideas that need further development, terms that need explanations, sentences that are awkward or unclear, and words that are inaccurate or misspelled. In other words, you review your paper for all the elements that a paper needs to be successful: content, style, grammar, and mechanics. You also check that the paper is written on an appropriate level for your readers, that it fulfills the purpose for which it was designed, and that it meets all of the expectations your readers have.

As you can see, reviewing a paper to correct any weaknesses is an important part of the writing process. It can also be a time-consuming step, so allow enough time to do a good job. Fortunately, you have a number of places to look for help. Let's look now at several opportunities you have to review your paper.

Your Review

Obviously, the first place to start your review is to read your paper yourself to note changes you want to make. In fact, you will need to reread and mark your paper many times, because each time you review it you will see additional changes that you want to make. Here are two suggestions that you may find helpful:

1. Allow time to elapse between your writing and your review. You will read your paper with a more objective eye once you have gotten away from it for a while, perhaps a day or longer.

2. Review your paper several times, each time for a different purpose. One review may be to check for content and organization, another review may be for grammar and sentence structures, and a third review might be for spelling and punctuation.

(Keep in mind that three reviews often are not enough!)

Peer Review

Once you have reviewed the paper yourself, you may be ready to get the advice of your friends and classmates. We call this type of help "peer review." Peer reviews may be a class activity, as your instructor will direct, or they may be informal help you and your friends exchange outside class. When you have a friend review your paper, ask him or her to read the paper and then give an honest, helpful evaluation of your paper—what is good about it and where it needs more work.

The Writing Lab

Another place to go for help with your paper is the writing lab of your college or university. Visit the writing lab and inquire about the services it offers. All writing labs have trained tutors who will work with you to revise and improve your papers. Some writing labs also hold sessions for small groups of students, focusing on grammar, spelling, test taking, and other useful skills.

On most campuses, you must make an appointment with a tutor well before you visit the writing lab. Some labs may allow walk-in visits, depending on the availability of tutors. If possible, you should schedule a visit to the lab at least once for every major writing assignment. Once you become familiar with a tutor, you may request that tutor each time you visit the lab. Remember to take the writing assignment and your textbook on your visit.

THE WRITING LAB   **EXERCISE 2.8**

Make an appointment with the writing lab to learn how the lab can help you with your papers for this course. As you plan your work for the term, schedule appointments for the times when you are most likely to need help with your papers.

Computer Review

When you write your draft at a computer, you have access to several tools to help you review and revise your paper. Perhaps the most obvious is the ability you have to revise text quickly and easily while seeing what you have written on the screen. You can make additions and deletions and rearrange the parts of your paper, all with the help of a few commands. When you have completed the changes you want to make, you can print out the new version right away.

Computers can help you improve your paper in other ways as well. A spelling checker will help you locate and correct misspelled words and typographical errors. The computer may also have grammar check programs or style analyzers, which some writers find useful. If you have access to such programs, experiment with them to see if they improve your writing.

COMPUTER AIDS   **EXERCISE 2.9**

Visit a computer lab on campus to learn what computers and software are available for your use. Then schedule some time in the lab so that you can become familiar with these tools.

Your Instructor's Help

After exploring all of these avenues for help with reviewing and revising your paper—self-review, peer review, the writing lab, and computer aids—you may want to schedule an appointment with your instructor to discuss your paper. Here are some suggestions for a good working relationship with your instructor:

1. Set up an appointment with your instructor that is convenient to both of you, and then be on time for the appointment. If you must miss an appointment, inform the instructor in advance.

2. Arrive at your appointment with your paper and specific questions to ask your instructor. As an alternative, your instructor may be willing to read your paper in advance of the appointment.

3. Never ask your instructor to proofread an entire paper to mark grammatical and mechanical errors. At this stage in your development as a writer of English, you should have developed ways to identify and correct these errors yourself.

4. Be respectful of your instructor's time. While your instructor will be happy to work with you on your paper, he or she also has other students and other responsibilities.

REVISING YOUR PAPER: EASIER THAN BUILDING A HOUSE

We began this chapter comparing writing a paper with building a house: Both are step-by-step processes that begin with planning, move on to construction, and end with the finishing touches. But when it comes to making changes to improve the final product, what a difference between a paper and a house!

The joy of the writing process is that you have unlimited opportunities to rethink what you have written so far and to improve your paper in any way you choose. (It's too bad if you decide you don't like your house's floor plan after the walls are up. With a house, such drastic changes are nearly impossible to make.)

When revising your paper, you can even reevaluate decisions you made at the beginning of the writing process. Suppose that you originally planned to focus your paper on the need for more restrictions on smoking in public places to reduce the health hazards to those who smoke. After doing your research, you might decide that the danger of passive smoking to nonsmokers is a more serious problem because passive smokers are unwilling victims of others' actions. In this case, you could change the focus of your paper after you have begun your research or even written a draft of your paper.

In summary, with the process approach to writing you have many opportunities to rethink and change your paper so that the final manuscript represents your best work, your best ideas.

CHAPTER 3

Guiding the Reader

One of the characteristics of effective writing is **coherence.** Coherent writing is well organized; the readers can follow the train of thought and see how the sentences and paragraphs fit together.

Think of your paper as a forest of words. Although you are familiar with the paths through this forest, your readers are not. If you don't provide the correct signs, your readers may get confused and lost. In a paper, the signs you provide include the thesis statement, paragraphing, and transitions.

This chapter reviews these important parts of a paper to show you how to make your papers more coherent. The chapter includes a section on introductions and conclusions. Introductions help you to state the topic and purpose of your papers while gaining the interest of your readers. Conclusions give you another chance to remind the readers of what you have said in the paper. As with thesis statements, paragraphing, and transitions, introductions and conclusions help to guide readers through your paper. The chapter also includes a brief review of outlining, because an outline is a good way for you to check that your paper is organized in a logical manner and that you have enough details to support your main points.

THESIS STATEMENT

A paper puts forward a writer's point of view. This point of view, also called a **thesis statement,** is the main idea of the paper. It is usually stated near the beginning of a paper.

Here are some thesis statements from student papers included in this chapter:

> In my opinion, the problem of childhood malnutrition in Latin America could be resolved by giving people an adequate education, improving public services, and having more committed politicians. (Jorge Ayala)

> Japanese products dominate the world market because the Japanese are hard working, technologically oriented, and diligent in their efforts to improve products. (Ko Yeu-Ying)

Some thesis statements also *forecast* the paper's organization. In the first thesis statement, Jorge Ayala forecasts that he will discuss three ways to eliminate childhood malnutrition in Latin America. A forecasting thesis statement indicates the paper's main points and its organization. When you read Ayala's paper, you will see that he devotes a paragraph to each solution to malnutrition, in the order forecast in the thesis statement.

In another paper included in this chapter, Roy Braine uses two sentences for his thesis statement:

> What causes hunger in third world countries? The answer lies in politics, overpopulation, and primitive ways of agriculture.

The readers of Braine's paper know that he will discuss these causes of hunger in the order he has listed in the thesis statement.

A word of caution here. In all the thesis statements discussed so far, the writers have forecast that they will discuss *three* topics. You need not always have three topics to support a thesis statement. You could have one, two, four, or five. For example,

> To understand the Arab–Israeli conflict, we need to consider the views of both the Israelis and the Palestinians.

Readers of this paper will expect the writer to discuss two topics, the views of the Israelis and the views of the Palestinians.

In the example that follows, note how the forecasting thesis statement connects to the topic sentences of the second and third paragraphs.

HUMAN FACTORS: A MAJOR CAUSE OF FAMINE

Tetsuya Okita

According to recent research, the number of famines does not appear to decrease with the advance of technology. Most people believe that famines are caused by droughts or floods, factors beyond human control. But they are wrong. Droughts and floods cause famines when coupled with man-assisted disasters. I believe that a major cause of famine is human factors such as civil wars and government mismanagement.

First, civil wars can cause famines. Take a country like the Sudan, which experienced drought for a few years. When the civil war broke out, millions of Sudanese died of starvation. This is because the United Nations (UN) and other food suppliers were cut off by the war. For example, the Red Cross suspended all flights to Sudan because all the landing in areas held by the Sudan Peoples' Liberation Army (SPLA) had been bombed by the government (Prendergast 32). However, in Botswana, which faced a ten-year drought in the 1980s ("The Horn is Empty" 38), nobody died of starvation, mainly because the country did not have a civil war. Relief food could be transported easily by road or by air.

Second, government mismanagement can be a major cause of famine. For example, Ethiopia could actually feed itself, since more than half of the country's arable land is being cultivated. But . . .

ANALYZING THESIS STATEMENTS   **EXERCISE 3.1**

1. Analyze the following thesis statements. Make a list of the topics you would expect to find in the paper in which each thesis statement appears. Then compare your lists with those of a partner. Discuss the similarities and differences in your lists.

   The major problems faced by international students in the United States are the language barrier and different customs.

   The most important alternative energy sources are nuclear power, solar power, and hydropower.

   Nuclear power offers a number of advantages, but it also involves risks.

2. Can you improve any of these thesis statements to clarify the topics?

PARAGRAPHING

Another feature of a coherent paper is unified, well-organized paragraphs. A paragraph is a unit dealing with a single idea. This idea is stated in a **topic sentence,** which is usually placed at the beginning of the paragraph. The rest of the sentences in the paragraph expand and support the topic sentence with evidence such as facts, statistics, examples, and quotations.

The indentation which marks the beginning of a paragraph signals to the reader that a new idea is going to be introduced and that the idea is going to be expanded and later supported with evidence. Consider the following paragraph in Roy Braine's paper:

> Another factor that causes hunger in the third world is overpopulation. Although in 1983 the agricultural production in India increased more than in previous years, India had to feed 80 million more mouths, causing a severe problem to government and offsetting the balance between consumption and production (Dumont 35). In 1978–79 China's agricultural production increased sharply due to decollectivization and the greater application of fertilizer, but this was offset by the rapid increase in population. As a result, several laws had to be passed to control the rising population (Dumont 35).

In the preceding paragraph, the topic sentence "Another factor that causes hunger in the third world is overpopulation" introduces the idea the paragraph deals with. To support this idea, Braine cites evidence in the form of comparative statistics for India and China.

In the following paragraph, Jorge Ayala introduces the main idea of the paragraph (inadequate education as a cause of malnutrition) in the first sentence of the paragraph. He then uses personal experiences as illustrations to support this point.

First of all, with an adequate education, people will come to realize the importance of a balanced diet for a child. In fact, a lot of people in Latin American countries do not realize the importance of a balanced diet. It reminds me of something I've heard from a number of people from Latin American countries. They told me that their grandparents still believe that a fat child is a healthy child. Actually, many fat children have health problems such as tooth and skin diseases, which are related to malnutrition. Certainly these problems are less likely to happen with educated people, who have learned the importance of eating foods that supply us with different nutrients.

Some writers use a **question–answer** technique, posing a question in the topic sentence and providing answers in the following sentences. The following paragraph uses the question–answer technique.

How credible is an institution like the International Monetary Fund, which carefully monitors the efficient use of loan funds administered to poor countries for development, but neglects to curb military expenditure? It is ironic that while many third world countries have been forced to reduce health and education budgets, they have been allowed to more than quintuple their military spending since 1960. The reason is simple: trading in weapons with poor countries is a $50 billion a year business. (Quino Gonzalez)

A question can be an effective way to begin a paragraph, as in the preceding example. However, you should not begin too many paragraphs this way; too many questions at the beginning of paragraphs would seem monotonous. A question at the beginning of one paragraph is probably enough for a paper.

EXERCISE 3.2   PARAGRAPHING

The following passage contains three paragraphs. Where should paragraphs two and three begin?

Perhaps the most obvious natural event that has caused famine in the Third World is drought. When droughts occur in succession, people die from starvation. For instance, at the end of the 19th century, there were three massive food crises, each of which probably caused millions of deaths. The first disaster, the "Great Famine" of 1876–78, was especially intense in parts of India. Then, India was devastated by two more famines in 1896–97 and 1899–90. The main cause of these famines was drought. South Asia gets most of its rain during the southwest monsoon season which blows from June to October. The grains are planted at the start of the monsoon and harvested about six months later. Failure of the monsoon rains can mean widespread crop losses, reduction in food availability, and famine. Another natural event that has caused famine in the Third World is floods. For example, the cyclone that tore into the southeastern coast of Bangladesh last year was the worst storm to hit that nation in twenty years. Winds up to 145 mph drove a 20-foot-high tidal wall of water over a dozen low-lying islands and into the mainland. This tidal wave drowned over 150,000 people and left more than nine million people homeless. Bangladeshi officials asked for help from other countries in order to feed the survivors and to prevent the spread of disease. The relief effort was difficult to carry out as much of the region was still flooded. Ships were unable to dock because the storm had washed away docks and jetties in the islands. The survivors faced a threat of famine because their rice crop was ruined, three-quarters of their livestock had died, and all their fishing boats were broken. In addition to droughts and floods, earthquakes can also cause famines. For example, last year, a massive earthquake ripped through northern Iran. Houses and apartment buildings collapsed, crushing thousands of people under mounds of rubble. Entire towns and villages were destroyed. Hostile terrain made rescue efforts very difficult. In addition, bad weather hindered cargo planes and helicopters from airlifting supplies to the region. The people in these parts faced a famine because the earthquake had also damaged vital irrigation systems and destroyed agriculture in an area known as Iran's "breadbasket." (Tetsuya Okita)

TRANSITIONS

Transitions, which are another way to make your papers coherent, link your ideas together. Transitions can be used between sentences, paragraphs, and major sections of your paper. Their purpose is to show the relationship between two ideas: how the second idea follows logically from the first, and how both are related to your thesis, which is the main idea of your paper.

To see how transitions can make a paper more coherent, read this paragraph about Japan's labor. Then read the same paragraph with transitions.

Paragraph without Transitions

The Japanese can develop highly profitable products because their labor is technologically oriented. Many Japanese work as engineers, technicians, or scientists, or some other occupation related to technology and production. Many Japanese students choose to major in high-tech fields instead of the humanities mainly because high-tech is more profitable than the humanities. The U.S. is less materialistic than Japan. Many college students pursue their dreams instead of profits, majoring in the fine arts, history, and philosophy. Many Americans work in the areas of humanities and social work. Only a small percentage of the Japanese population work in these areas. (Ko Yeu-Ying)

Paragraph with Transitions

Secondly, the Japanese can develop these highly profitable products because their labor is technologically oriented. *For example,* many Japanese work as engineers, technicians, or scientists, or some other occupation related to technology and production. *Moreover,* many Japanese students choose to major in high-tech fields instead of the humanities for the simple reason that high-tech is more profitable than the humanities. *In comparison,* the U.S. is less materialistic than Japan. Many college students pursue their dreams instead of profits, majoring in the fine arts, history, and philosophy. *In addition,* many Americans work in the areas of humanities and social work. *By contrast,* only a small percentage of the Japanese population work in these areas. (Ko Yeu-Ying)

As you can see, transitions can make a big difference in making a paragraph easy to follow.

Transitions that show the relationship between ideas in a paper take several forms. The most obvious is **transitional words and phrases.** Box 3.1 shows some transitional words and phrases, indicates their functions, and gives an example for each transitional word or phrase.

In addition to transitional words and phrases, **repetition of key words** helps to connect individual sentences and paragraphs. In the following paragraph from Ko Yeu-Ying's paper, the key word *work* is repeated to keep the reader on track.

First of all, we know that the Japanese *work* hard, often sacrificing their free time to their jobs. According to one report, the Japanese *work* an average of 42 hours per week while Americans *work* an average of 35 hours a week. These hours certainly increase Japanese productivity and at the same time create a highly competitive society. This hard *work* contributes to the incredible growth of their industries, which have overtaken industries in the U.S.

Sometimes, as in the following paragraph from Jorge Ayala's paper, the first sentence may function as a transition as well as a topic sentence.

In addition to improving people's education, the problem of childhood malnutrition can be diminished by improving public services. I would like to

---

Transitional Words and Phrases   **BOX 3.1**

To show cause: therefore, thus, consequently

> ESL students must study hard to master courses taught in English. *Therefore,* they have little free time.

To tell time: later, then

> First I must read the assignment, and *then* we can discuss it.

To tell place: below, above, on the left

> The oak tree is near the entrance to the library. *Below* the tree is a bed of daffodils.

To summarize: in conclusion, in summary

> *In conclusion,* I hope we can find a way to ensure peace in this troubled region.

To add: also, in addition, further

> I want to go to Florida to visit Disneyworld. I would *also* like to visit the NASA Space Center.

To enumerate: first, second

> The *second* problem I had with my car was bad brakes.

To compare/contrast: similarly, however, on the other hand, in contrast

> We expected the weather to be cold. *However,* the temperature did not fall below 76 degrees.

To illustrate: for instance, for example

> There are many ways to make a paragraph coherent. *For instance,* you could start with a topic sentence.

---

recall something that has happened in many Latin American countries, the spread of cholera.

The topic sentence reminds the reader of the idea discussed in the previous paragraph (the need for improved education) and introduces another way to solve childhood malnutrition—improved public services.

Transitions, as you have seen, make a paper more coherent by showing us how ideas are related and how the paper is organized. However, you should avoid using too many transitions, especially too many transitional words and phrases such as those in Box 3.1. Sometimes the relationship between ideas is obvious without the use of transitions. The paragraph below is easy to follow, but it doesn't use a single transitional word or phrase listed in Box 3.1.

The dispute between Arabs and Israelis over Palestine dates back to the beginning of the 20th century, when the area was under British rule. The first step towards the armed confrontations was the "Balfour Declaration" in 1917, which gave the Jews the lever for claiming Palestine as their own territory. By 1925, about 34,000 Jews had immigrated to the traditionally Arab area, and when their number doubled in 1936, the first clashes between the immigrants and Palestinians occurred. The declaration of the State of Israel in 1948 and its expansion in the West Bank of the Jordan River and the Gaza Strip during the Six-Day War of 1967 left the Palestinians homeless. (Pavlos Louca)

EXERCISE 3.3   **USING TRANSITIONS**

Fill in the blanks in the following paragraphs with suitable transitions. The transitions are given at the end of the paragraph.

Paragraph 1:

In another example, the United States required Japan to open its beef and orange markets a few years ago, and Japan complied. _____, the United States is also requiring Japan to open its rice market now. Some U.S. congressional representatives say that Japan's trade practices are unfair, _____ the United States has 17 restricted agricultural products and Japan has only 13 such products. _____, Japan will have to open its rice market soon because of U.S. pressure. _____ Japan is the second largest economic power, the Japanese government, which has no political muscle, has to accept the demands of the U.S. government.

[**transitions:** however, although, because]

Paragraph 2:

Despite several rounds of talks between the two ethnic groups in Cyprus, the Greek Cypriots and the Turkish Cypriots, no agreement has been reached. _____, the 1992 peace conference led by the Secretary-General of the United Nations offers the best chance of a solution to the problem. _____, the two groups have serious disagreements that make the task of the United Nations harder. _____, in my opinion, a solution can be achieved only if both groups are willing to make some concessions on territorial and constitutional issues.

[**transitions:** however, therefore, accordingly]

Paragraph 3:

Second, government mismanagement can be a major cause of famine. _____, Ethiopia could actually feed itself, since more than half of the country's arable land is being cultivated. But, in 1988, the government sold nearly all the grain reserves to earn foreign exchange for weapons purchases. _____, millions of Ethiopians died in the famine which lasted from 1989 to 1991. _____, in the mid-1980s, _____ Kenya faced a drought as severe as the one that led to Ethiopia's great famine, it only faced local food shortages. This is _____ the Kenyan government had acknowledged the problem early and imported enough grain to feed its people.

[**transitions:** because, on the other hand, for example, as a result, but, although]

FINDING EXAMPLES OF TRANSITIONS   EXERCISE 3.4

Find examples of these kinds of transitions from an article in *Time* or *Newsweek:*

    a transitional word or phrase

    repetition of a key word

    a topic sentence that also functions as a transition

OUTLINING

As you have probably realized from your other courses, an outline is often a good way to identify the main ideas of an article or a chapter in a book. Outlining can also be a good way to see the organization of a paper that you or someone else has written. When you outline your own papers before writing the first draft, you can plan the arrangement of ideas so that they are in logical order. You can even include the transitions and topic sentences in your outline to ensure your paper's coherence.

Shown below is an outline of the paper by Ko Yeu-Ying. The topic sentence is included as part of the outline. The paper is included in its entirety at the end of this chapter.

JAPAN: THE NEW SUPERPOWER

Thesis Statement: Japanese products dominate the world market because the Japanese are hard working, technologically oriented, and diligent in their efforts to improve products.

I. First of all, we know that the Japanese work hard, often sacrificing their free time to their jobs.
   A. Comparison of Japanese work week with U.S. work week
   B. Productivity and industrial growth

II. Secondly, the Japanese can develop these highly profitable products because their labor is technologically oriented.
   A. Example—technological occupations in Japan
   B. Japanese students' choices of majors
   C. Contrast—U.S. students' majors and occupations

III. Finally, the Japanese do extensive research in Japan and other countries to improve their products.
   A. Investments in U.S. research universities
   B. Research results in better products

IV. Conclusion

INTRODUCTIONS AND CONCLUSIONS

Good papers begin and end well; that is, they have effective introductions and conclusions. Good introductions and conclusions are not always easy to write. In fact, many writers often revise and rewrite these two sections many times before they are satisfied. Here are a few suggestions that will help you to write these important parts of your paper.

Introductions

The first few sentences of your paper are especially important because they are the first impressions that your readers will have about the paper and about you, the writer. To be effective, the introduction, which usually is the first paragraph of your paper, should

- state the topic of your paper,
- state the purpose of your paper, and
- gain the interest of your readers.

Although this may look difficult to achieve, note that almost all the student writers whose papers are included in this book have written introductions that stated the topic and purpose of their papers while also gaining your interest. Here are some suggestions on writing effective introductions.

Stating the Topic of Your Paper

Stating the topic is easy to do, since the thesis statement is usually included in the first or second paragraph of your paper and the thesis contains the topic of your paper. Most of the papers included in this book state the thesis (and the topic) at the end of the first paragraph. By writing a clear thesis statement, you also will state your topic clearly.

Stating the Purpose of Your Paper

By purpose, we mean your reason for writing the paper. Since the purpose is important to you, you should indicate it to the readers so that they know your paper is worth reading. The purpose is often implied in the thesis; if not, it could be stated elsewhere in the introduction.

For example, in the introduction to his paper titled "Surviving in Cambodia," included in its entirety in Chapter 6, Ponh Lanh states that his purpose is to explain how he survived the hardships in Cambodia while millions of Cambodians died.

> The Civil War in my country, Cambodia, ended in 1975. At that time, I was nine years old. From 1975 till 1979, I lived under Communist rule. Within these four years, many children around my age died of starvation. As for me, I survived through the entire four years by knowing how to lie and how to steal.

Gaining the Interest of Your Readers

Think of yourself as a reader. What makes you want to read a news story, a research paper, or a book? It could be an interesting headline, an unusual title, or a striking statistic in the introduction. In your papers, you could use similar techniques to catch the readers' attention.

For instance, in Chapter 8, Nita Bavikati titles her paper "Meiji, Mother of Modern Japan." Since the term "Meiji" may not be familiar to many of us, we could be interested in reading her paper. In addition to the title, Bavikati uses striking statistics to keep us interested.

> The sixties was a comfortable time for the United States. American companies prospered to no end, supplying "over three-quarters of the

television sets, half the motor cars, and a quarter of the steel used around the world" ("High Technology" 3). However, something went terribly wrong in the next two decades. The American trade balance "went from a surplus of $5 billion in 1960 to a deficit of $150 billion in 1985" ("High Technology" 3). What went wrong? The answer lies with a group of small islands in the Pacific known as Japan. Today, Japan is considered an industrial giant, exceeded in industrial strength only by the U.S. and Russia.

In the same chapter, Faisal Hussain also uses statistics in the introduction to gain our interest in his paper titled "AIDS in Africa and Asia."

According to the World Health Organization (WHO), nearly 70 percent of the people infected with AIDS live in Africa (see Figure 1). Countries with a high rate of infection are Uganda, Burundi, Malawi, Rwanda, Tanzania, and Zambia (Weeks 208). WHO also reported that in 1992, Asia had 1 million individuals, mostly in India and Thailand, whose blood had tested positive for the AIDS virus (Steele 11). The fatal disease has spread over these continents quickly in the past ten years and the potential impact over the next decade could be devastating.

In their introductions, writers use various techniques to lead in to the thesis statement. Lanh used a few sentences describing the situation in Cambodia, and Bavikati and Hussain used interesting statistics. In addition to these techniques, some writers use a question in their introductions to lead in to the thesis statement. Syed Arafat Kabir uses this technique in his paper titled "Women's Place in Islam," which also appears in Chapter 8.

Is there any accepted human rights code in this world? The answer is yes. It constitutes freedom of speech and freedom of choice regardless of race and gender.

If you are writing on an unusual topic, you may have to provide readers with an extended definition in the lead-in. Amir K. Shafi does this in his paper titled "Women of the Veil: Happy or Oppressed?" in Chapter 8.

Purdah comes from a root word meaning veil or curtain. It refers to the custom of secluding women and enforcing certain high standards of female modesty. It is the usual explanation given for the absence of Muslim women in public places. This practice dates back from the time of the Prophet Muhammad. Others claim it did not take hold until the eighth century when a profligate ruling class began to hide their innumerable wives and concubines from public view. In any event, purdah has been a custom in the Muslim world for fourteen hundred years (Warwick 462).

✓ The introduction need not be just one paragraph; when you read Bavikati's paper in Chapter 8, you will see that her introduction is two paragraphs long and that the thesis statement is placed at the end of the second paragraph.

Conclusions

As with introductions, many writers revise and rewrite their conclusions several times before they are satisfied. The conclusion is important because it is your last chance to remind the reader of what you have said and, in the case of argumentative papers, your last chance to convince the reader of your position on an issue. Some writers believe that the conclusion should be a summary of their paper or a restatement of the thesis statement. This is true of longer papers, such as Assignment 3 in this book. But, even for longer papers, do not repeat the thesis statement word for word.

What, then, is an effective conclusion? To a large extent, the conclusion depends on the purpose of your writing. If, for instance, you were writing a lab report, the purpose would be to report on what you learned during an experiment. Accordingly, in the conclusion section of the lab report, you would describe what you learned by conducting the experiment and analyzing the data. If you began your paper by asking a question, as Syed Arafat Kabir did, you should provide an answer to the question by the time the conclusion is written. On the other hand, if you began your paper by stating a problem, you should offer a solution by the time you conclude the paper. In fact, in some papers, the plan for your entire paper should include the conclusion. That is, before writing a paper that asks a question or states a problem, you should have the conclusion in mind.

Remember that the conclusion does not have to be long. We have already seen how Ponh Lanh began his paper titled "Surviving in Cambodia." He concludes the paper effectively with just three sentences:

> Many people died during that four years of living under the Communist rule. These people died of starvation and from not knowing how to talk their way out of a bad situation. As for me, I survived because I knew how to lie and how to steal.

In "Meiji, Mother of Modern Japan," Nita Bavikati concludes her paper as follows:

> In conclusion, Japan's initial modernization at social, economic, and political levels was due to the Meiji period. Imagine that the Meiji era never existed. Would Japan still have maintained its complete isolationist policy? Would Japan be a little known, underdeveloped Third World nation? Of course, this is just supposition, but it merits speculation.

She quickly restates her thesis (her paper is fairly long) but leaves us with an interesting speculation.

Faisal Hussain, after analyzing the hard facts and statistics concerning AIDS in Africa and Asia, concludes that the

WHO and other organizations are fighting continuously against AIDS in Africa and Asia. However, considering the rate at which AIDS is spreading, the battle may already be lost.

EXERCISE 3.5 **ANALYZING INTRODUCTIONS AND CONCLUSIONS**

Analyze the following introductions and conclusions. Are they effective? Why or why not? Be specific in your responses.

Example 1:

Third World countries have many problems that industrialized countries have learned to solve a long time ago. One of these problems is the early death of many infants. In my country, Honduras, many children in the rural areas die before reaching one year of age. This is due to three basic situations that plague the poor, uneducated society of my country.

In conclusion, many rural children will die each year due to the inexperience of their mothers and the lack of medicines and medical equipment. I hope that in the future the government makes the necessary changes to save the rural children, since the children of today are the future of tomorrow.

Example 2:

The happy and feminine notes of an old song are carried by the wind and echoes through the forest. The voices of other women, who are also washing clothes or bathing their children in the river, join the melody. Their wide hips, that were many times opened to bring life, move to the rhythm of the song. Their strong arms rub hard on the clothes against big river stones while their children play with the suds.

This has been a typical scene of Latin American women for half a century, and can still be seen in rural areas. Although they may not show it, these women have been the victims of poverty, male chauvinism, and other social problems for many years.

Poor, rural women in Latin America are the victims of a long tradition of exploitation. However, they continue to perform the central role in their families.

Example 3:

Is there any accepted human rights code in this world? The answer is yes. It constitutes freedom of speech and freedom of choice regardless of race and gender. However, in the Muslim world, some women are not being given their fair share of rights. The situation can best be described in the words of an Iranian lecturer who says that "It is easy to live as a woman in Iran as long as you first accept that you are worth half a man" ("Cover up" 30). The root of this deprivation can be traced back to the legal structure of the Muslim world and its traditional values and beliefs.

In the 1930s Picasso painted an Algerian woman "with the hall open and sunlight streaming in" (Fernea 7). What Picasso wanted to show on canvas was that Muslim women of Algeria were experiencing a life of prosperity and well-being. The picture is, however, different now although the world has advanced in every sphere. That may be why the Algerian writer Assia Djebar hopes that the view of Picasso will be the future of Muslim women (Fernea 12), the sunlight being education, freedom of speech, and choice; and the open door being the changed social order and a more realistic legal structure. In conclusion, one can only wish that Djebar's hope will be fulfilled in the future.

WRITING A SHORT ESSAY   EXERCISE 3.6

Write a short essay on one of the following topics. Begin with a thesis statement, which *may* forecast the main topics you will discuss in the paper. Be sure to include a topic sentence for each paragraph as well as transitions and repetition of key words to make your essay coherent.

problems you face as an international/ESL student

your happiest experience

your goals for the next 5 years

what you like (or dislike) about your academic major

READINGS

For the papers that follow, consider these study questions:

1. What do you like about these papers?
2. Do you think these papers are coherent? That is, can you follow what the writers are saying? If so, identify the techniques the writers used to make the papers coherent. If the papers have problems with cohesion, how can the writers improve them?
3. Are there places where you wish the writers had added more information? Did the papers leave you with questions that the writers had not answered?

4. Write an outline of paper 1 and paper 3, following the model for "Japan: The New Superpower" on page 44. Identify the thesis, the topic of each paragraph, and details used to support these topics. Do the writers use the first sentence of a paragraph to introduce a new topic? Do some topics have more than one paragraph?

5. Write the thesis statement of paper 1 and paper 3.

6. Write the topic sentence of the second paragraph in paper 1 and paper 3. Does the information in the paragraph relate to the topic sentence? If not, explain.

7. Write the topic sentence of the third paragraph in paper 1 and paper 3. Does the information in the paragraph relate to the topic sentence? If not, explain.

Paper 1

CHILDREN'S MALNUTRITION IN LATIN AMERICA

Jorge Ayala

Many Latin American countries confront social, political, and economic problems. One of the problems that this region suffers is malnutrition in children. In my opinion, the problem of childhood malnutrition in Latin America could be resolved by giving people an adequate education, improving public services, and having more committed politicians.

First of all, with an adequate education, people will come to realize the importance of a balanced diet for a child. In fact, a lot of people in Latin American countries do not realize the importance of a balanced diet. It reminds me of something I've heard from a number of people from these countries. They told me that their grandparents still believe that a fat child is a healthy child. Actually, many fat children have health problems, such as tooth and skin disease, which are related to malnutrition. Certainly these problems are less likely to happen with educated people, who have learned the importance of eating foods that supply us with different nutrients.

In addition to improving people's education, the problem of childhood malnutrition can be diminished by improving public services. I would like to recall something that has happened in many Latin American countries, the spread of cholera. Cholera is transmitted by contaminated water and food. Of course, it can be avoided by treatment of the water supply, but in many Latin American countries water and food supplies are not always clean. I remember a small town in Panama that I visited a few years ago. In that town, the water supply comes from a river. Sometimes a little chlorine is added to treat the water. During droughts, people get water from small streams and wells, which are contaminated. As a result, many children in that town experience stomach problems, which are caused mainly by contaminated water, and tooth decay, which is caused by lack of fluoride in the water.

More committed decisions by politicians may improve the life style of the people. This can be illustrated by a problem caused by multinational companies. It sometimes appears that the only objective of such companies is to keep people poor in order to get cheap workers. In fact, this was clearly seen in my former town, where the people have spent their whole life on tobacco production for a multinational company. Even though they work very hard, they do not get enough money for three complete meals a day or to buy adequate food for their children. We suspect that many multinational companies are under the protection of the government, because the companies have paid for election campaigns in the past. On the other hand, conscientious politicians would make decisions to benefit all the people of the country.

In conclusion, many children in Latin American countries will continue to suffer from malnutrition due to lack of parental education, inadequate public services, and lack of committed politicians. I hope one day Latin American governments realize the importance of healthy children to society.

Paper 2

JAPAN: THE NEW SUPERPOWER

Ko Yeu-Ying

With the breakup of the Soviet Union and the U.S. economy just coming out of a recession, Japan is in line for superpower status. Japanese high-tech consumer products have come to dominate the world market, including the American domestic market. "Made in USA" has sometimes been replaced by "Made in Japan" as a mark of a quality product. In fact, Japanese products dominate the world market because the Japanese are hard working, technologically oriented, and diligent in their efforts to improve products.

First of all, we know that the Japanese work hard, often sacrificing their free time to their jobs. According to one report, the Japanese work an average of 42 hours per week while Americans work an average of 35 hours a week. These hours certainly increase Japanese productivity and at the same time create a highly competitive society. This hard work contributes to the incredible growth of their industries, which have overtaken industries in the U.S.

Secondly, the Japanese can develop these highly profitable products because their labor is technologically oriented. For example, many Japanese work as engineers, technicians, or scientists, or some other occupation related to technology and production. Moreover, many Japanese students choose to major in high-tech fields instead of the humanities for the simple reason that high-tech is more profitable than the humanities. In comparison, the U.S. is less materialistic than Japan. Many college students pursue their dreams instead of profits, majoring in the fine arts, history, and philosophy. In addition, many Americans work in the areas of humanities and social work. By contrast, only a small percentage of the Japanese population work in these areas.

Finally, the Japanese do extensive research to improve their products, in Japan as well as in foreign countries. For example, well-known Japanese companies support research at top U.S. universities like MIT, Stanford, and Cal Tech. The Japanese will use this research to produce more high-quality products.

In summary, the Japanese can dominate the world market, including the American domestic market, because of their work ethic and technological orientation. As a result, high-quality Japanese products have spread to every corner of the world.

Paper 3

HUNGER IN THE THIRD WORLD

Roy Braine

"In a sprawling camp of mud and cardboard hovels in the outskirts of Khartoum, 2-year-old Rasha Abdul-Said Omar cries as she fingers a bowl of porridge" ("Sudan" 46). Rasha is one of the millions of children who suffer from hunger today. Hunger exists, especially in parts of Africa, where the famine of 1984–85 killed at least half a million people in Ethiopia ("Sudan" 46). What causes hunger in the third world countries? The answer lies in politics, overpopulation, and primitive ways of agriculture.

In some third world countries, politics has played a major role in causing hunger. In Sudan, for instance, the ruler Gen. Omar Hassan al-Bashir and his officers took an anti-Western stand in 1989. He blamed the relief workers for corruption and ignored warnings by the United Nations about the country facing a severe shortage of food ("Sudan" 46). Because of the ruler's anti-Western stand, thousands of people had to suffer. Another example of how politics could cause hunger is through civil war. This is the case in Ethiopia. Last May, the U.N. estimated that the war between the guerrillas and the government of Ethiopia blocked food from getting to 700,000 hungry people ("Alive" 50).

Although the U.S. and other Western countries report that they are helping third world countries to end hunger, statistics tell us a different story. For example, to end hunger in Africa, only $900 million worth of food and food transport aid is needed. But the U.S. and other powerful nations have done little to raise this money, which is less than a day's cost of the Persian Gulf War (Tang 361).

Another factor that causes hunger in the third world is overpopulation. Although in 1983 the agricultural production in India increased more than in previous years, India had to feed 80 million more mouths, causing a severe problem to government and offsetting the balance between consumption and production (Dumont 35). In 1978–79 China's agricultural production increased sharply due to decollectivization and the greater application of fertilizer, but this was offset by the rapid increase in population. As a result, several laws had to be passed to control the rising population (Dumont 35).

Another effect of overpopulation can be seen in Bangladesh, where land is lost to population growth (Boyce 476–77). Because of this, landless people are increasing in Bangladesh. Furthermore, the population of India will be 40 percent higher and the population of the Philippines will be 50 percent higher in the year 2025, which will result in high environmental and economic costs that will halt development in these countries (Karaosmanoğlu 35). In summary, high population increases will cause more problems for poor countries, because their budgets are not enough to cope with the increase. This means that more and more third world countries will be dependent on the West for help (Karaosmanoğlu 35–36). The future of the world hinges above all on whether or not we can curb the world's terrifying population explosion (Dumont 37).

The third cause of hunger in the third world is primitive agricultural methods. In Ethiopia, there are many more farmers than its poor land can support (Dumont 35). This means that pasture land and forests will be exploited more and more. Plowing too often can reduce the soil's fertility, and plowing natural pastures and forests will cause a major reduction in the rainfall and heavy soil erosion (Tang 361). In some countries, when the government has tried to improve agriculture, the results have not been positive. For instance, when Sudanese farmers were moved to new areas, their bonds of kinship and ties to the land were disrupted. Due to a lack of commitment, the replacement farmers have shown little interest in long-term development (Kantos 651). Further, in Sudan, "farm productivity is hampered by outmoded cultivating practices, unlike in most other developing countries" (Kantos 651). The result is famine.

In Bangladesh, however, new studies have shown that farmers who use new technology enrich the soil much better than farmers who don't. As a result, farmers who do not use new technology tend to produce smaller crops than farmers who do. For example, water could be pumped more efficiently with a water pump than with traditional methods (Alauddin and Tisdell 561–63). If hunger is to be curbed, traditional ways of farming will have to be replaced by new methods.

In conclusion, children like Rasha Abdul-Said Omar could be saved if only the people of the world cared to join to eliminate hunger. Droughts and floods need not cause famines. Famines occur because of poor "public policy which prevents governments, aid agencies, and private traders from meeting food shortages "("Bad Gets" 46). Most people who starve today live in Africa where "wars and government incompetence keep help away" ("Bad Gets" 46). The best way to stop famine is more help from countries like the U.S., education in population control, and the use of new machinery. Unless third world countries join together to solve their problems, the starving will keep on dying silently.

WORKS CITED

Alauddin, M., and C. Tisdell. "Poverty, Resource Distribution, and Security: The Impact of New Agricultural Technology in Rural Bangladesh." *Journal of Development Studies* July 1989: 550–67.

"Alive Another Year." *The Economist* 3 Dec. 1988: 50.

"Bad Gets Worse." *The Economist* 9 Nov. 1991: 46.

Boyce, J. K. "Population Growth and Real Wages of Agricultural Laborers in Bangladesh." *Journal of Development Studies* July 1989: 467–81.

Dumont, R. "The Coming Crisis." *World Press Review* Jan. 1990: 35–37.

Kantos, S. "Farmers and Failure of Agribusiness in Sudan." *Middle East Journal* Autumn 1990: 649–53.

Karaosmanoglu, A. "Challenge of Sustaining Growth with Equity in Asia." *Finance & Development* Sept. 1991: 34–37.

"Sudan: The 'Silent Dying.'" *Newsweek* 15 April 1991: 46.

Tang, I. "The Forgotten." *The Nation* 30 Sept. 1991: 361.

CHAPTER 4

Writing Clear Sentences

One of the most important characteristics of good writing is sentence clarity. Clarity is important for writing in your coursework and for writing you will do later on the job or in your profession. For ESL students learning to write academic papers in English, clear sentences are especially challenging. You want to communicate in a way that your instructors and classmates will understand, and of course you want to get full credit on exams and papers for your knowledge and ideas. Yet you are writing in a language that you may not have completely mastered. You may still be learning the conventions of English grammar and syntax, as well as English vocabulary.

This chapter offers suggestions that will help you write clear sentences. It reviews some of the guidelines and rules for writing good sentences, including questions of style, such as sentence length and variety, and some of the most commonly made grammatical problems.

READING ENGLISH

As we discussed in Chapter 1, the best way to improve the fluency of your written English, other than practicing your writing, is to read in English as much as possible. The amount of English you read translates directly into your ability to write clear sentences, because as you read you absorb patterns of sentence structure, syntax, and vocabulary.

It is important that you find the time to read English as often as possible, beyond your textbook assignments. One way to do this is to find magazines or books on topics that interest you but that are not necessarily related to your coursework. You might enjoy reading about sports, your hobby, or current events. Or you might want to read fiction.

A READABLE STYLE

One way to write with clarity in English is to use sentences that are interesting and easy to understand. Precise, descriptive word choices contribute to readable sentences, as do sentence structures that are simple, varied, and direct. Let's begin by discussing sentence length and variety.

Sentence Length and Variety

Sometimes the biggest obstacle to writing with clarity is that the writer tries to include too many ideas in one sentence. In fact, this problem can occur with the writing of native English speakers as well as with the writing of ESL students.

Sentences that are too long and complicated are difficult to read, and they're difficult to construct correctly. So our first tip for writing clear sentences is to *keep them short.* Limit every sentence to the expression of one or two ideas. If you find yourself getting tangled up in a sentence or find that it's getting too long, stop and divide it into shorter sentences.

What's a long sentence? This question doesn't have a definite answer, but a rule of thumb might be about 15 words. Can an effective sentence ever be longer than 15 words? Of course. In fact, it's a good idea to vary the lengths of your sentences so that your writing doesn't become monotonous. The important point to remember is that, as a general rule, your sentences should be under 15 words. If you have had trouble with sentence structures in the past, see if one problem might be that you are trying to include too many ideas in one sentence.

Sentence variety, including sentences of different lengths, is another tip for writing papers that people want to read. If all sentences are about the same length or have similar structures, the result is monotonous, boring writing that quickly lulls the reader to sleep. So include some short sentences and an occasional longer one (but make sure the longer sentences are easy to understand). And vary the way your sentences are constructed. Write in simple sentences, compound sentences, and complex sentences. Also vary the way your sentences start. Begin some with introductory phrases, such as transitional expressions or adverbial clauses. Here are some examples of varied sentence beginnings:

We studied four hours for the test.

Therefore, we studied four hours for the test.

Because the material was difficult, we studied four hours for the test.

A good way to check for the variety of your sentence lengths and structures is to read your papers aloud. Notice when your voice pauses for sentence endings or commas. The goal is to avoid regular, repetitive patterns, patterns that are described in English as "sing-song."

EXERCISE 4.1   REVISING SENTENCES FOR VARIETY

Two long sentences are given below. Rewrite them as shorter sentences using a variety of lengths and structures.

But with high unemployment, as Western Europe has today, strong nationalism and criminality tend to grow and immigrants become a target for those who need to have someone to blame for being without a job and for having the same social benefits.

Because alternative energy sources such as solar, wind, and hydrogen fuel are showing their potential to replace petroleum and coal, countries and utility companies are encouraged to increase their research funding and investments in alternative energy sources in order to improve efficiency and utilize more nonpolluting energy sources.

Direct Sentences

Another way to write clear sentences is to make them as direct as possible. In other words, say what you mean simply and concisely.

Writing in active voice is usually a good way to write direct sentences. With **active voice,** the subject of the sentence performs the action described by the verb:

I wrote the paper last night.

In this sentence, the subject *I* performs the action *wrote*.

Here are some additional sentences written in active voice:

Silvia chose to major in electrical engineering.

Fadzil returned the books to the library.

The research team conducted the experiment.

The opposite of active voice is passive voice. In a **passive voice** sentence, the subject is acted on by another agent, which may or may not be named in the sentence. Here are the preceding sentences written in passive voice:

Electrical engineering was chosen by Silvia as a major.

The books were returned to the library by Fadzil.

The experiment was conducted by the research team.

Sometimes the agent of a passive voice sentence may not be identified in the sentence:

The computer was broken.

The students were asked to review the lab procedures.

In the first sentence, we are not told who broke the computer. In the second, we are not told who asked the students to review the lab procedures.

As a rule, sentences written in the active voice are more concise and readable than passive sentences, and they may also contain more complete information. Suppose you returned to your room after classes and found this note on your door:

> Your car has been borrowed, and it was wrecked.

Wouldn't you want to know who borrowed and wrecked your car? The sentence on the note is written in passive voice, and it leaves out essential information. Why do you think the writer wrote in passive voice?

While it is often better to write in active voice, sometimes passive voice is acceptable if the agent is unknown (this may be the case for the note about the car) or if the agent is unimportant:

> New safety regulations have been issued to reduce lab accidents.

In this sentence, it may not be important to know who issued the regulations.

For most of your sentences, though, write in active voice. Direct, active sentences will make your writing clear.

COMMON GRAMMATICAL PROBLEMS

Writing clear sentences also requires you to learn the rules of English grammar and mechanics such as the correct use of verbs and pronouns, as well as commas and other marks of punctuation. These rules give most students trouble, whether English is their first or second language. In fact, as an ESL student you may have an advantage over native speakers, because you have studied the language formally. Some native speakers of English have not had the intensive training in grammar that you may have had in your study of English as a second language.

English grammar is a complicated matter, as is the grammar of any language. It is thus beyond the scope of this book to cover grammar completely. What we will look at here are some of the grammar problems that seem most common in the writing of ESL students (and often the writing of native speakers as well).

Speakers of some languages or language groups may have special problems with English grammar. This is because some languages have characteristics that are not found in English, or English may have characteristics that are not found in other languages. For example, speakers of Romance languages such as Spanish, French, and Italian may note the following differences between their language and English.

- In Romance languages, adjectives are usually placed after the noun they qualify (Spanish: *un libro interesante*). In English, adjectives are usually placed before the nouns (an interesting book). As a result, speakers of Romance languages may place adjectives after the noun when they write in English.

- In Romance languages, comparatives and superlatives are usually formed by using *more,* such as *more tall.* English has *more interesting* as well as *tall, taller,* and *tallest.*

- Double negatives are allowed in Romance languages. As a result, speakers of Romance languages may use double negatives when they write in English. In English, double negatives are usually not allowed.

- In Romance languages, the present tense is often used to indicate future action: *Next week, I go to San Antonio.* In English, this sentence is normally written as *Next week, I will go to San Antonio.*

- Spanish is the only Romance language that uses the progressive tense, such as *She is studying.* Speakers of French and Italian may therefore have a problem in showing the differences between the simple and progressive tenses when they write in English.

- In Romance languages, a noun may have a grammatical gender. For example, in Spanish, *table* (*la mesa*) is feminine and *tree* (*el arbol*) is masculine.

Speakers of some Asian languages, such as Chinese, Japanese, and Korean, may note the following differences between their language and English.

- These languages *may not* have the definite (*the*) and indefinite (*a, an*) articles. As a result, when speakers of these languages write in English, they tend to omit articles or add too many.

- Plural forms of nouns are rarely used in these languages.

- Verbs are not usually conjugated for tense, person, and number. In English, verbs are always conjugated. For example:

He *runs* every day.

He *ran* yesterday.

They *run* every day.

- In Japanese, the subject is often omitted from sentences.

- Vietnamese does not indicate plurality.

Speakers of Slavic languages, such as Polish and Russian, may note the following differences between their language and English.

- In Slavic languages, definite and indefinite articles are not usually expressed.

- In these languages, double negatives are usually allowed.

- Slavic languages permit a somewhat loose word order. As a result, speakers of these languages may mix up the word order when they write in English.

- Slavic-language speakers may have difficulty in using countable and uncountable nouns because the differences between *much* and *many* and between *few* and *little* are not clear to them.

Arabic, another language spoken by a large number of ESL students, uses the definite article (*the*) more often than English does. Thus, Arabic speakers tend to overuse the definite article when they write in English.

British and American English

Many ESL students are from countries where British English is spoken. Because British English and American English have many differences, these students may have problems mainly with vocabulary (words), spelling, and punctuation.

Vocabulary

These problems are of two types. First, the same word may have different meanings. For example, in British English, *to table* something is to bring it forward for action, such as a proposal at a meeting; in American English, *to table* has the opposite meaning. In British English, *homely* means simple or informal; in American English, it means plain or unattractive.

The second problem in vocabulary is that British and American English use different words for the same object. The following list includes a few of these words.

British	*American*	*British*	*American*
aerial	antenna	ground floor	first floor
autumn	fall	lift	elevator
bill	check	nappy	diaper
biscuit (sweet)	cookie	petrol	gas
car bonnet	hood	post box	mail box
car boot	trunk	shorthand typist	stenographer
car park	parking lot	solicitor	attorney
chips	french fries	trunk call	long-distance call
cupboard	closet		
full stop (punctuation)	period	underground	subway
		work out (problem)	figure out

Spelling

The main differences in British and American English spelling are as follows:

-t/-ed (in the past tense)   British English uses *-t,* as in *burnt* and *learnt;* American English uses *-ed,* as in *burned* and *learned.*

-re/-er   Some British English words end in *-re,* such as *metre, theatre,* and *centre.* In American English, these words end in *-er,* such as *meter, theater,* and *center.*

-ae/-oe   In British English, many words (especially scientific terms) are spelled with the long vowel *ae*—for example, *diarrhaea, aesthetic,* and *gynaecology.* In American English, the long vowel is shortened to *e,* as in *diarrhea, esthetic,* and *gynecology.*

Punctuation

QUOTATION MARKS   In British English, single quotation marks are used first. For quotes within quotes, double quotation marks are used:

> At the beginning of class, the teacher asked, 'Have you read the chapter "Writing to Persuade," which was assigned for today?'

In American English, quotation marks are used in reverse order:

> At the beginning of class, the teacher asked, "Have you read the chapter 'Writing to Persuade,' which was assigned for today?"

In British English, commas and full stops are placed *after* the final quotation mark:

> The new student said, 'I must telephone my parents'.

In American English, commas and periods are placed *before* the final quotation mark:

> The new student said, "I must telephone my parents."

COMMAS IN LISTS   In British English, listed items are written without a comma before *and:*

> Tom, Harold, Jane and Paula

In American English, a comma may be inserted before *and:*

> Tom, Harold, Jane, and Paula

Major Sentence Errors

Major sentence errors of ESL students include comma splices, fused (or run-on) sentences, and sentence fragments. These errors can create serious problems because they may make your writing difficult for your readers to understand. Therefore, it is important to eliminate major sentence errors from your writing.

Comma Splices

Comma splices occur when two independent clauses are joined by a comma alone. An *independent clause* is a group of words with a subject and a complete verb; it is called an independent clause because it could stand alone as a sentence. Here are some examples of independent clauses:

> I will graduate after two more years.
> Then I will return to China to begin my career as a pharmacist.

Each of these clauses can stand alone as a sentence, or they can be combined. If we combine them with only a comma, we will have a comma splice:

> I will graduate after two more years, then I will return to China to begin my career as a pharmacist.

We can correct this comma splice in several ways. The first is to replace the comma with a semicolon:

> I will graduate after two more years; then I will return to China to begin my career as a pharmacist.

We can also correct the comma splice by adding a coordinate conjunction after the comma. Coordinate conjunctions are as follows: *and, but, or, nor, yet, so, for.* Here is the correction:

> I will graduate after two more years, and then I will return to China to begin my career as a pharmacist.

Finally, we can correct the comma splice by making one of the clauses dependent (or subordinate). *Dependent clauses* begin with subordinate conjunctions or relative pronouns. Subordinate conjunctions include *when, after, because, although, since.* Relative pronouns are as follows: *whom, whose, what, whoever, whichever, whatever, who, which,* and *that.*

Here are several ways to correct the comma splice by making one of the clauses dependent:

> After I graduate in two more years, I will return to China to begin my career as a pharmacist.

> Because I will graduate in two more years, I can then return to China to begin my career as a pharmacist.

> Although I won't graduate for two more years, I plan then to return to China to begin my career as a pharmacist.

Here is a comma splice that can be corrected using a relative pronoun:

Comma Splice:

My roommate spends many hours in the library, she is planning to go to graduate school.

Corrected:

My roommate, who is planning to go to graduate school, spends many hours in the library.

Fused Sentences

Another major sentence error, which is similar to a comma splice, is a fused (or run-on) sentence. In a **fused sentence,** two independent clauses are joined without any punctuation at all. Here are examples of fused sentences:

My dormitory is very noisy I am looking for another place to live.
I have enjoyed studying in this country I miss my family.

Fused sentences like these are usually easy to recognize and correct. They are corrected in the same ways you correct a comma splice. Remember that both comma splices and fused sentences can be written as two separate sentences.

Sentence Fragments

A **sentence fragment** is just what its name suggests: a part (fragment) of a sentence. Some essential part of the sentence may be missing, such as a complete verb. For example:

The students in the library. (This group of words lacks a verb.)

The students who are studying in the library. (*Are studying* is a complete verb, but it is in a dependent clause: *who are studying in the library.*)

Although, many students were studying in the library. (*Although* is a subordinate conjunction, making this group of words a dependent clause. *Although* cannot substitute for *however,* although the two words have similar meanings.)

Sometimes fragments occur when the writer uses an incomplete verb phrase, such as a present participle:

The reason being that I have too much homework tonight.

This sentence can be corrected by replacing the present participle (*being*) with a complete verb (*is*):

The reason is that I have too much homework tonight.

To avoid sentence fragments, be sure that you write in independent clauses containing a subject and a complete verb. Can you correct these fragments?

The man in the red sweater.

For example, my roommate from Jordan.

These fragments can be corrected in many ways, all of them requiring that the writer provide additional information. Here are possible corrections:

The man in the red sweater is my next-door neighbor.

For example, my roommate from Jordan spends five hours a day on his English homework.

EXERCISE 4.2   CORRECTING SENTENCE ERRORS

Correct the following sentences, which contain comma splices, fused sentences, and sentence fragments.

1. My dormitory is very noisy, I am looking for another place to live.
2. Dr. Ruiz explained the homework problems to us, she is our calculus teacher.
3. I have enjoyed studying in this country, I miss my family.
4. My roommate spends many hours in the kitchen she loves to cook.
5. Because I hope to be an electrical engineer.
6. My roommate being too lazy to help with the cleaning.
7. For example, the six students who recently arrived from Russia.
8. The opportunities in my country for well-trained engineers are exciting I have chosen to be a civil engineer.
9. I spend long hours in the library therefore my research paper should contain important information.
10. I studied thoroughly, thus I made an A.

Problems with Verbs

Two other problems in ESL students' papers are verb tense and verb agreement. This section reviews some of the most important rules for correct verb usage, although you may also need to review additional rules and examples in a comprehensive grammar handbook.

Verb Tense

The **tense** of a verb is related to the time when the action takes place. The most fundamental tenses (times) are past, present, and future.

Past Tense:

When I was five years old, I *moved* to Pakistan.

Last night my roommate and I *ordered* pizza.

I *tripped* on the stairs as I *came* to class.

Present Tense:

I *hope* to make a good grade in this course.

I *am studying* my history textbook now.

Does your friend *like* this university?

Future Tense:

Tonight *we will* go to the movies.

Next quarter I *will take* a computer course.

I *will be finished* with these problems soon.

Other important tenses are past perfect and present perfect. With past perfect, the action described in the verb took place in the past before something else occurred.

Past Perfect:

Because I *had studied* English for many years in India, I found my ESL classes easy.

After Juan *had completed* his homework, he watched television.

He drove the car away after it *had been repaired.*

Present perfect verbs describe action that began in the past and continues into the present:

Present Perfect:

I *have been* in the United States for three years.

New computers *have been installed* in the lab.

The dog *has run* around the block five times.

There are additional verb tenses other than the ones reviewed here, but these are the ones you probably will use most often in your writing. The key is to use the tense that fits the time you are writing about.

Verb Agreement

Verb agreement means that the verb you use agrees with the subject in number: Singular subjects take singular verbs and plural subjects take plural verbs.

Singular:

One student is standing under the tree.

Nasr studies every night.

She likes to play tennis on the weekends.

Plural:

Three students are standing under the tree.

Nasr and Alan study every night.

They like to play tennis on the weekends.

Agreement can be particularly tricky if a group of words comes between the subject and the verb. In the following sentences, the subject and the verb are italicized. Notice how the phrases between them may interfere with choosing the correct verb.

One of my best friends *is coming* to visit.

The *flask* sitting on the shelf with the large beakers *belong*s in this cabinet.

The *children* sitting in the park with their mother *are eating* ice cream.

Verbs are the heart of any sentence, so it's important to use them correctly. When revising your writing, check that you have used the right tenses and that your verbs agree with their subjects.

EXERCISE 4.3   CORRECTING VERB TENSE AND AGREEMENT

In the paragraph that follows, many of the verbs are incorrect in tense and agreement. Identify the verbs and correct the sentences.

Nuclear power are very necessary for Singapore. Situated right in the middle of South East Asia, Singapore was a small island with a land area of only 639 square kilometers. With no natural resources, Singapore have to depend on power-generating plants to meet its energy requirements. However, since 1961 when the country gain independence, the country have been transformed from a small trading nation to a modern economy with a high standard of living. Electricity was currently being generated at four power stations with a total generating capacity of 4,133 megawatts. In 1991, the demand for electricity is about 16,600,000 kilowatt-hours; however, only 16,596,000 kilowatt-hours will be produced.

Thus, the electricity generated was barely sufficient to meet the requirements. Any increase in demand for electricity resulted in serious problems for Singapore. Instead of using power plants, an alternative source which generated a large amount of power at low cost is found.

Problems with Pronouns

Pronouns, like verbs, give problems to many writers. Two of the most common problems are pronoun reference and pronoun agreement.

You may remember that a pronoun refers to (or stands for) a noun. The noun that the pronoun refers to is called its **antecedent.** Here are examples of clear and unclear pronoun reference:

Lydia gave her assignment to the professor. (In this sentence the pronoun *her* refers to the antecedent *Lydia*.)

The computer lab was closed when he arrived. (This sentence doesn't identify the antecedent of the pronoun *he*. Probably a previous sentence has identified who *he* is. If not, then this sentence has a problem with unclear pronoun reference, which is discussed next.)

Pronoun Reference

To avoid problems with **pronoun reference** in your papers, be sure that your readers know the *antecedent* of every pronoun you use. They should recognize the antecedent easily.

Antecedents of personal pronouns (like *he, her, I,* etc.) are usually clear, but three pronouns may cause problems in students' papers: *which, it,* and *this*. Of these three, the word *this* causes problems for many writers. Read these sentences:

After studying for three days, Annie took the chemistry test. This was a new experience for her.

What is a new experience for Annie? Possibilities include *studying for three days* or *taking a chemistry test*. We can't be certain because the reference of the pronoun *this* is unclear.

Another way to describe this pronoun problem is to say that the reference is broad, vague, or ambiguous. Here is another example:

The problem with working full-time while you take a full course load is that it takes too much time.

What takes too much time—working or taking a full course load? The antecedent of the pronoun *it* is not clear. In reality, the pronoun probably refers to the combination of activities that is too time-consuming, but the reader can't be certain of the writer's intended meaning.

Here's a final example of ambiguous pronoun reference:

Last night for supper I ate pizza and ice cream, which made me gain twenty pounds, I'm sure.

What are the possible antecedents of *which*?

Be sure that the references of all your pronouns are clear so that your readers don't have to guess what you mean. Be particularly careful with *this, which,* and *it.*

Pronoun Agreement

Another common pronoun problem is agreement. The rule for **pronoun agreement** is simple: A pronoun should agree with its antecedent. This means singular nouns take singular pronouns, and plural nouns take plural pronouns:

The boy dropped his book.

The boys dropped their books.

Pronouns also should agree with the gender (masculine, feminine, or neuter) of their antecedents:

The boy talked with his professor.

The girl took her notes to the library.

But what would you do about the following sentence?

Each student should turn in (his, her, their) homework.

The pronoun *their* is not correct, because *student* is singular. But is the antecedent masculine or feminine? You can't tell from this sentence.

Until about a decade or so ago, writers of English would use the masculine pronoun (*he, his, him*) if the gender of the antecedent was unknown. Today many people no longer consider this usage to be acceptable, although the alternative isn't always easy to see. One solution is to use plural antecedents:

All students should turn in their homework.

Sometimes, writers use one of these alternatives:

Each student should turn in his or her homework.

Each student should turn in her or his homework.

Each student should turn in his/her homework.

Each student should turn in her/his homework.

The correct use of gendered pronouns can be a sensitive topic with some people, so be careful in your writing to avoid problems in using them. When you revise your papers, check that you have used pronouns properly, including correcting any errors in pronoun agreement and reference.

CORRECTING PRONOUN PROBLEMS   **EXERCISE 4.4**

Rewrite the following sentences to ensure correct pronoun reference and agreement.

1. If the computers do not work, the lab assistant should note its serial number on the daily report sheet.
2. After the dog bit Takashi, he complained to campus police; they issued a warning to his owner.
3. Ruth is taking five courses and working at the library. This is difficult for her.
4. Lee told Ken that he deserved a raise.
5. The student newspaper has improved recently. They have fewer mistakes in spelling and grammar.
6. Last quarter, I took three extra courses and all required labs and research papers. This ruined my social life.
7. Each student scheduled a conference with their advisor.
8. Each student majoring in computer science should consult the department chair about his degree plans.
9. Alicia wrote letters to her family and studied for her calculus test, which she enjoyed.
10. The teacher required it to be written.

CHAPTER 5

Developing a Portfolio

For this course, you will write three major papers, all based on a single research topic. The papers build on each other. First, you will select a topic from the list in this chapter. For Assignment 1, you will express your knowledge and opinions on the topic you have chosen. You will then write a research proposal explaining how you will develop the topic for Assignment 2: Writing to Inform and Assignment 3: Writing to Persuade.

The papers you have written in response to the three assignments, and the research proposal, form a writing portfolio. A writing portfolio is thus a record of all the writing you have done for a course.

In Chapter 6, "Writing from Experience," you will learn to write a paper on the topic you've chosen by using your own knowledge and experience. Chapter 7 will show you how to summarize, paraphrase, and quote directly, and how to document your sources. In Chapter 8, "Writing to Inform," you will learn to use information from other sources, such as information you find in the library, to develop the research topic. Chapter 8 also includes sections on methods of development such as definition, and classification. In Chapter 9, "Writing to Persuade," you will learn the techniques of academic argument in preparation for Assignment 3.

As already mentioned, all the writing in this course will be based on a research subject you select. Some subjects are listed below. In addition to these subjects, your teacher may assign special subjects for your class. Read your choices carefully. Then select a subject that you can narrow to a topic for your paper. (See Chapter 2 for help with narrowing a subject to a topic.)

RESEARCH SUBJECTS

1. **Nuclear Issues** Both nuclear power and nuclear weapons play an important, but controversial, role in modern society. What are the advantages and disadvantages of using nuclear power? Are nuclear weapons a deterrent to conflict? Some new countries, formerly part of the Soviet Union, and some Third World countries now have nuclear weapons. What are the effects of this nuclear proliferation?

2. **AIDS in Africa and Asia** Although the AIDS crisis in the United States has received much media attention, the disease in Africa and Asia has received little notice until recently. Yet millions are already infected in some East African countries. In Asia, Thailand may have 5 million HIV cases by the year 2000. In India, an estimated 4,500 people are infected each month in Bombay alone. What causes the rapid spread of AIDS in

some African and Asian countries? Superstition? Indifference? What can be done to slow the epidemic in these countries?

3.   The New Superpower For years, many Third World countries benefited as a result of the power play between the two superpowers. With the Soviet Union defunct, the United States is the only superpower left. How does the new role affect the United States? How does the new role for the United States affect Third World countries? Will there be a new superpower? Will it be a united Europe or Japan?

4.   Ethnic/Religious Violence Despite the democratization that is sweeping the world, many societies are torn by ethnic or religious violence. Extreme nationalism and religious fanaticism are on the rise. What causes this violence? Has it affected your country? Is there a solution?

5.   The Status of Women They are presidents and prime ministers, doctors and engineers. In the past 50 years, women have made impressive gains, socially, politically, and economically. However, many women, from Western as well as Third World countries, still face discrimination, male chauvinism, and religious intolerance. What is the status of women in your home country? What advances have they made recently? What problems do they have yet to overcome?

6.   Cigarette Exports Americans are smoking less, so the tobacco industry is turning to Asia. Taiwan, Japan, Korea, and Thailand have opened their markets to American cigarettes. The industry's next target is China and its 1 billion population. The American tobacco industry is accused of targeting women and youth in these countries. Is the accusation true? If so, what are the long-term effects of targeting these women and youth? What can be done?

7.   Coming to America Thousands of international students arrive in the United States every year. Many of these students are away from home for the first time, in a setting that is quite different from theirs. What social and psychological problems do these students face? What is "culture shock"? What have colleges and universities done to help these students integrate with their new surroundings? What more can be done to help them?

EXERCISE 5.1   SELECTING A TOPIC

Reread the list of possible subjects just given as well as any additional subjects your instructor has provided. From this list, select two that you might like to work on for this course.

Next, review the techniques for narrowing subjects into topics and generating ideas (such as listing, clustering, and freewriting) discussed in Chapter 2. Use one or two of these techniques to generate ideas for the two subjects you are considering.

Finally, select the one topic that you will continue to work on for the course. Base your choice on your interests and the depth (and variety) of ideas you were able to generate.

SAMPLE PORTFOLIOS

To show how Assignments 1, 2, and 3 build on each other, we have included the writing portfolios of Zhiling Liu and Ragnhild Olsen. These writing portfolios include the students' papers from Assignments 1, 2, and 3, their research proposals, and their working bibliographies.

Portfolio 1—Zhiling Liu

For Assignment 1: Expressing Knowledge and Opinions

NUCLEAR POWER PLANTS

Zhiling Liu

With the economic development around the world, the shortage of the existing natural resources has become a severe problem. More and more countries are beginning to recognize the importance of energy and are trying to solve this crisis in different ways. Nuclear power plants are one way of producing more energy, although their use raises many controversial questions.

Nuclear power plants have three major advantages. The first is that they can supply a large amount of electricity by using relatively small amounts of fissionable fuel. Coal-burning plants, in contrast, consume thousands of tons of coal to supply electricity. The second advantage is that nuclear power does not produce air pollution. However, coal-burning plants pollute the air with dark and dense smoke and release terrible chemical smells. The third advantage is that nuclear power plants can provide stable electric current to those areas that face a shortage of electricity. For example, the proposed nuclear power plant in Da-Ya-Wan, Shenzhen, which is located in the southern part of Canton, China, will have the potential to supply electricity to Canton.

Canton, which is my hometown, is the center of economic and cultural life in the larger area of Guangdon and has had a power shortage for years.

During the summer, there are at least two days per week of no electricity. This blackout is necessary to supply enough electricity to the industrial companies. As a result, we have to suffer from the extremely high temperature because modern electronics such as air conditioning and electric fans do not work. Our lives are also affected. We do not go out as usual. Most of us have to stay at home.

I remember one summer night when I was doing my homework and suddenly the lights went off. I stopped working and expected electricity to resume soon. I did nothing but lie down on the bed for two hours. I couldn't fall asleep because it was so hot. I tried to cool down by using a hand fan. Once I stopped, I was sweating again. I got out of the bed at last and found a candle and a box of matches in the drawer. I finished my homework under dim candle light at 11:45. My eyes were so tired that I had to go to bed. Later, I found out it was past midnight when the electricity came back on.

In spite of the advantages of nuclear power plants, they also have some disadvantages that create a lot of questions. One is that the costs of building nuclear power plants are very high. In order to prevent radiation from escaping, a reactor needs some special materials to shield the core. The second disadvantage is that it costs a large amount of money to buy fissionable fuel. Disposal is the third problem. Nowadays, the waste is usually buried under the sea in some special containers. It is certainly not a good way to dispose of these radioactive wastes. The fourth problem is the possibility of human error, like the nuclear power plant accident in Chernobyl.

In 1986, the world's worst nuclear accident occurred in Chernobyl in the former Soviet Union and caused severe radioactive pollution of the environment. The residents had to leave the polluted area. Many people needed medical care after the leak. The radioactive dusts affected every local resident's health to some degree. This nuclear accident shocked people all over the world. As a result, people began to change their attitudes and began to lose confidence in nuclear power plants.

In conclusion, nuclear power plants are not perfect. While they benefit people, nuclear power plants can also threaten people's safety. However, if nuclear power plant workers are educated, the possibility of accidents will be greatly reduced. In my opinion, in the long term, building nuclear power plants will help to solve the world's energy crisis and will allow the world's economic development to continue.

Research Paper Proposal

RESEARCH PAPER PROPOSAL

Zhiling Liu

Thesis Statement: Nuclear power should be abandoned because of its potential risk to humans and the environment.

In Assignment 2, I will provide statistics about the effects of the Chernobyl disaster. For example, about 135,000 people were evacuated from the polluted area. I will also provide statistics about health problems suffered by the victims of the Chernobyl disaster. For example, thyroid cancers have increased. I will also show the reason for the crisis at Three Mile Island.

In Assignment 3, I will support my thesis statement by showing the dangers of such problems as human error and waste disposal. I will suggest that nuclear power be replaced by other forms of energy.

WORKING BIBLIOGRAPHY

Coble, Charles. *A Look Inside Nuclear Energy*. New York: Macmillan, 1989.

Duderstadt, James, and Chihiro Kikuchi. *Nuclear Power*. Ann Arbor: U of Michigan, 1979.

Fenn, Scott. *The Nuclear Power Debate*. New York: Praeger, 1981.

"Grim Fallout from Chernobyl." *Time* 14 Sept. 1992: 17.

Howe, Geoffrey. "Risk of Cancer Mortality in Populations Living Near Nuclear Facilities." *Journal of the American Medical Association* 20 March 1991: 1438–49.

Pringle, Laurence. *Nuclear Energy*. Milwaukee: Rain Tree, 1983.

Richardson, Harry. *Economic Aspects of the Energy Crisis*. Lexington: Saxon House, 1975.

Sorenson, Harry. *Energy Conversion System*. New York: Wiley, 1983.

Study Group Sponsored by the Ford Foundation. *Energy: The Next Twenty Years*. Cambridge: Ballinger, 1979.

"Ukraine to Keep Chernobyl Operation." *New York Times* 22 Oct. 1993: A8.

For Assignment 2: Writing to Inform

THE PROBLEMS OF NUCLEAR ENERGY

Zhiling Liu

As a result of the Three Mile Island accident in the United States and the Chernobyl accident in the former Soviet Union, people have realized the danger of nuclear power plants. Nuclear accidents, which sometimes result from poor management, can damage the environment and threaten the health of people, and safe disposal of radioactive wastes is difficult.

The Three Mile Island accident and the Chernobyl accident resulted from poor management. In September 1977, at a nuclear energy plant near Toledo, Ohio, a problem with the plant's cooling system was found but corrected before an accident could occur. Later, two inspectors reported the same kind of problem at the nuclear plant which was on Three Mile Island in Pennsylvania. Unfortunately, their warnings were overlooked (Pringle 30–31). As a result, a small amount of radioactive gas was released into the atmosphere. No one was hurt, but people were scared because they knew the accident could have been worse and threatened their lives (Coble 31).

The accident at Chernobyl, according to Bunyard, was due to many operating violations by the engineers (41). The engineers broke several safety rules in order to run an experiment. This shows that plant workers and even some managers lack a full understanding of how to operate nuclear power plants safely (Kapitza 7). Administrators and engineers at power plants in the Soviet Union were hired more for political reasons than for their technical expertise and education (Kapitza 7). Operating failure and overconfidence of the engineers caused a release of radioactivity into the air. "The explosion and the fires that followed sent 12 million curies of the most dangerous forms of radioactivity into the environment during the first twenty-four hours" following the accident (Pringle 65). Although the Soviet government took many steps to prevent the release of radioactivity, "[T]he estimate is that 20 percent of the radio-iodine . . . and about 12 percent of the radio-caesium" in the core escaped (Bunyard 35).

In the Chernobyl accident, radioactivity not only polluted the air of the Soviet Union but also the air in European countries such as Britain, Greece, and Sweden. According to Bunyard, the Soviet government evacuated 135,000 people who lived around the disaster zone. Livestock were also removed in order to protect them from radioactivity (34). In Britain, sheep farmers claimed they had a loss of $15 million because their sheep were affected by radioactivity and were banned by the British government from the domestic market (Bunyard 37).

Radioactivity also damaged people's health. According to a report in *Time*, "[o]ne of the most disturbing predictions following the near meltdown of the Chernobyl nuclear power plant on April 26, 1986, was that cancer cases would eventually begin to rise in the area affected by the fallout from the accident" ("Grim Fallout" 17). In the Soviet state of Belarus, Chernobyl radiation caused a sharp increase in thyroid cancers, especially among children ("Ukraine" A8).

Even if accidents can be avoided, the safe disposal of radioactive waste is difficult. After the Chernobyl accident, "helicopters . . . [dumped] some 5,000 tonnes of material into the burning core . . . and 1,800 tonnes of clay and sand to help seal off the fire" and debris (Bunyard 34–35). Like the Chernobyl debris, radioactive wastes which are produced by nuclear power plants remain a threat for thousands of years to both people and the environment (Coble 32). As Coble says, "Radioactive strontium 90 and cesium 137 [waste products of nuclear power plants] have half-lives of around 30 years. A small percent of plutonium 239 is also present [and] its half-life is over 24,000 years" (Coble 32). Radioactive waste can damage the environment. Cesium-137, for example, can be absorbed from the soil by plants, which may be eaten by human beings and livestock.

Since the Three Mile Island accident and Chernobyl accident, the percentage of people against nuclear power has dramatically increased. People say they are scared to live in areas close to the nuclear power plants. Others argue "that energy priorities should be conservation and development of clean, renewable, nonnuclear technologies" (Fenn 19). Since management, environment, public health, and radioactive wastes present long-term problems which require scientific research, in my opinion, we should work to develop other forms of energy.

WORKS CITED

Bunyard, Peter. "Nuclear Energy After Chernobyl." *Earth Report*. Ed. Edward Goldsmith and Nicholas Hildyard. Los Angeles: Price Stern, 1988. 33–50.

Coble, Charles. *A Look Inside Nuclear Energy*. New York: Macmillan, 1989.

Fenn, Scott. *The Nuclear Power Debate*. New York: Praeger, 1981.

"Grim Fallout from Chernobyl." *Time* 14 Sept. 1992: 17.

Kapitza, Sergei P. "Lessons of Chernobyl: The Cultural Causes of the Meltdown." *Foreign Affairs* 72.3 (1993): 7.

Pringle, Laurence. *Nuclear Energy*. Milwaukee: Rain Tree, 1983.

"Ukraine to Keep Chernobyl Operation . . ." *New York Times* 22 Oct. 1993: A8.

For Assignment 3: Writing to Persuade

NUCLEAR ENERGY IS NOT THE ENERGY OF THE FUTURE

Zhiling Liu

With the economic development around the world, the shortage of existing natural resources has become a severe problem. More and more countries are beginning to recognize the importance of energy and trying to solve this crisis in different ways. Nuclear power plants are one way of producing more energy. However, as a result of the Three Mile Island accident in the United States and the Chernobyl accident in the former Soviet Union, people have realized the danger of nuclear power plants. Nuclear accidents, which sometimes result from poor management, can damage the environment and threaten the health of people; safe disposal of radioactive wastes is difficult; and the spread of nuclear power plants increases the danger of nuclear terrorism.

The Three Mile Island accident and the Chernobyl accident resulted from poor management. In September 1977, at a nuclear energy plant near Toledo, Ohio, a problem with the plant's cooling system was found but corrected before an accident could occur. Later, two inspectors reported the same kind of problem to the nuclear plant which was on Three Mile Island in Pennsylvania. Unfortunately, their warnings were overlooked (Pringle 30–31). A small amount of radioactive gas was released into the atmosphere. No one was hurt, but people were scared because they knew the accident could have been worse and could have threatened their lives (Coble 31).

The proponents of nuclear energy say that one of the best ways to solve the shortage of the existing natural resources is to build nuclear power plants. It is true that nuclear power plants can produce more energy, and it is true that a shortage of energy can seriously affect cities and people. Consider the shortage of electricity in my home town, Canton. The proposed nuclear power plant in Da-Ya-Wan, Shenzhen, which is located in the southern part of Canton, will have the potential to supply electricity to Canton, which is the center of economic and cultural life in the larger area of Guangdon and has had a power shortage for years. During the summer time, there are at least two days per week of no electricity. This blackout is necessary to supply enough electricity to industrial companies.

Although a nuclear power plant could supply stable electric current to Canton, a release of radioactivity would destroy my home town. As in the accident in Chernobyl, where people suffered from the radioactive release, I believe my family and relatives would also face the same situation. Nuclear power plants produce more energy and consume less resources than many other forms of power plants, but nuclear power plants also threaten people and the environment, as the Chernobyl accident shows.

The accident at Chernobyl, according to Peter Bunyard, was due to many operating violations by the engineers (41). On April 26, 1986, the engineers broke several safety rules in order to run an experiment. This illustrates that plant workers and even some managers lack a full understanding of how to operate nuclear power plants safely. Managers and workers at nuclear power plants in the Soviet Union were often hired for political reasons instead of for their knowledge of nuclear power plant operations (Kapitza 7). At Chernobyl, operating failure and overconfidence of the engineers caused a release of radioactivity into the air. "The explosion and the fires that followed sent 12 million curies of the most dangerous forms of radioactivity into the environment during the first twenty-four hours" following the accident (Pringle 65). Although the Soviet government took many steps to prevent the release of radioactivity, "the estimate is that about 20 percent of the radio-iodine in the core escaped and about 12 percent of the radio-caesium" escaped (Bunyard 35).

In the Chernobyl accident, radioactivity not only polluted the air of the Soviet Union but also polluted the air in European countries such as Britain, Greece, and Sweden. According to Bunyard, the Soviet government evacuated 135,000 people who lived around the disaster zone. Livestock were also removed in order to protect them from radioactivity (34). In Britain, sheep farmers claimed that they had a loss of $15 million because their sheep were affected by radioactivity and were banned by the British government from the domestic market (Bunyard 37).

Radioactivity also damaged people's health. According to a report in *Time*, "cancer cases would eventually begin to rise in the area affected by fallout from the accident" ("Grim Fallout" 17). And the *New York Times* reports that in the Soviet state of Belarus thyroid cancer increased at an alarming rate, especially among children ("Ukraine" A8).

Although proper management and qualified employees might reduce the number of nuclear power accidents, human beings are not perfect, and even a small mistake can have catastrophic effects. For example, in March 1975, at the Browns Ferry Nuclear Power Plant in Decatur, Alabama, a fire was accidentally set under the inspector room by a technician who was using lighted candles to check for air leaks. Although the fire was controlled immediately, "electric controls [were] burned out and water [fell] to a dangerously low level" (Sweet 92). In March 1978, at the Rancho Seco reactor in California, "a technician dropped a small object into the control panel . . . causing [the reactor to] go nearly out of control for an hour" (Sweet 97). Human error is unavoidable, but the consequence of human error in a nuclear power plant can be disastrous.

Even if accidents can be avoided, the safe disposal of radioactive waste is difficult. After the Chernobyl accident, "helicopters . . . [dumped] some 5,000 [tons] of material into the burning core . . . and 1,800 [tons] of clay and sand to help seal off the fire" and debris (Bunyard 34–35). Like the Chernobyl debris, radioactive waste, which is produced by nuclear power plants, must be stored for thousands of years so that it does not contaminate people or the environment (Coble 32). Some waste products of nuclear power plants have very long half-lives. The half-life of plutonium, for example, is over 24,000 years (Coble 32). Radioactive waste can be absorbed from soil by plants, which may be eaten by human beings and livestock.

Proponents of nuclear energy say that nuclear waste can be buried under the sea in special containers. However, burying this waste turns our world into a big, radioactive dumping ground. Although proponents of nuclear energy say that radioactive waste is buried in leak-proof containers, if leaks do occur, our future generations will be affected.

The spread of nuclear power plants also increases the danger of nuclear terrorism. Terrorists could steal either nuclear fuel or nuclear waste and build bombs which could threaten entire cities. Twenty years ago, the U.S. government organized a special team to fight nuclear terrorism. Since then, the team has investigated over 80 threats that were considered to be serious. All of the threats were false. But the danger still remains. Both nuclear reactor fuel and nuclear reactor waste can be converted into nuclear weapons. According to William Sweet, "[c]riminal organizations have a [proven] ability to recruit highly skilled manpower required to design and operate heroin plants" (184). If criminals can recruit experts to process heroin, criminals can recruit experts to build nuclear bombs. Proponents of nuclear power say that radioactive materials can be protected by effective security. But Paul Leventhal, who is the head of the Nuclear Control Institute, says that "a better approach [to control nuclear material] is to end the global commerce in plutonium" ("Preparing" E3).

From the above discussion, we can see that the potential threats of nuclear energy to human beings are rather serious. The world's economic development requires more and more energy. However, nuclear power is not worth the risk it poses to people and the environment. Nuclear power plant accidents could kill thousands of people and ruin millions of acres of land; and nuclear wastes, which also endanger people and the environment, are produced by nuclear power plants. In addition, radioactive material could be stolen from nuclear power plants and used by terrorists to build nuclear bombs. Nuclear energy is not the energy of the future.

WORKS CITED

Bunyard, Peter. "Nuclear Energy After Chernobyl." *Earth Report*. Ed. Edward Goldsmith and Nicholas Hildyard. Los Angeles: Price Stern, 1988. 33–50.

Coble, Charles. *A Look Inside Nuclear Energy*. New York: Macmillan, 1989.

"Grim Fallout from Chernobyl." *Time* 14 Sept. 1992: 17.

Kapitza, Sergei P. "Lessons of Chernobyl: The Cultural Causes of the Meltdown." *Foreign Affairs* 72.3 (1993): 7.

"Preparing to Meet Terrorists Bearing Plutonium." *New York Times* 1 Aug. 1993: E3.

Pringle, Laurence. *Nuclear Energy*. Milwaukee: Rain Tree, 1983.

Sweet, William. *The Nuclear Age*. Washington: Congressional Quarterly, 1988.

"Ukraine to Keep Chernobyl in Operation." *New York Times* 22 Oct. 1993: A8.

Study Questions for Zhiling Liu's Portfolio

1. What is Liu's thesis statement for Assignment 1?

2. What is the thesis statement for Assignment 2?

3. What is the thesis statement for Assignment 3?

4. Liu's opinion about the use of nuclear power changed after she had written Assignment 1. Why do you think she changed her view?

5. Notice the personal experience that Liu used to develop Assignment 1. Did she include personal experience in Assignment 2? Assignment 3? How did she change her use of personal experience in Assignment 3?

6. What main differences do you notice between Assignment 1 and Assignment 2?

7. What are the main differences between Assignment 2 and Assignment 3?

8. What do you like most about Liu's papers?

9. How do you think Liu's papers could be improved?

10. Do you have questions that you wish Liu had answered?

Portfolio 2—Ragnhild Olsen

For Assignment 1: Expressing Knowledge and Opinions

ETHNIC VIOLENCE IN EUROPE

Ragnhild Olsen

In Norway, we have had an increase of ethnic violence over the last couple of years between Norwegian citizens and recent immigrants. So far, this violence had taken place in our largest cities and mostly between young people. But the problem has grown larger and now involves older people too.

There are differences between Norwegians and immigrants because we have grown up in societies with a different culture and religion, which have had a strong influence on how we think and behave. Our languages are also barriers which make it harder to get to know each other. Even though these cultural differences are evident, the increasing ethnic violence in Norway can also be related to three other situations.

First of all, the system my country has built to integrate immigrants into our society is not good enough. It takes far too long for my government to decide who is going to get permission to stay in Norway. Meanwhile, the new immigrants have to wait in areas especially built for them. I studied with a girl from Iran who had been waiting six months at a place like this. Her family got enough food and other things, but the days could be very long and boring. This waiting period should have been used to teach our new Norwegian citizens about Norway, our language, and our culture.

Those who get permission to stay are moved to our largest cities where they get an apartment in a district where mostly immigrants live. They are of course allowed to move, but without a job it is expensive to afford anything else. It would have been much better if they had been placed at different locations and especially in areas where other Norwegians live. We would have been more used to seeing people from different countries in our neighborhood, and some of the problems we have because of our different ethnic backgrounds would have disappeared. However, today most of our immigrants live in the poorest part of our cities and hardly have any contact with Norwegians.

The next situation which can be a reason for the increased violence in my country is our economic situation and high unemployment. There will always be some Norwegians who have negative behavior towards foreign people, but with high unemployment, as we have today, strong nationalism and criminality tend to grow. As a result, immigrants become a target for those who need to have someone to blame for being jobless; they also envy the immigrants for having the same social benefits as us. Because of our high unemployment, the Norwegians' attitudes toward immigrants are often negative. Most of this negative attitude is based on insufficient knowledge about our immigrants' backgrounds and traditions. This will improve if we receive more information about their cultures and become more integrated with our new citizens.

We cannot blame only our immigrant policy and our economic situation for the increased violence in Norway today. Our new citizens have to try to do the best they can to become familiar with our culture. It is important to hold on to one's own traditions, culture and religions, but to some extent the immigrants should adapt to the society they live in now. For example, I saw a program on television about a boy from India who lives in Norway with his family. He had problems getting friends because his parents wouldn't allow him to interact with Norwegian teenagers.

There are no easy solutions to the increased ethnic violence in Norway, but if we have a chance to do more things together, we will learn about each other's culture and build more respect for the differences between us.

Research Paper Proposal

RESEARCH PAPER PROPOSAL

Ragnhild Olsen

<u>Thesis Statement</u>: The increasing ethnic violence in Western Europe can be connected to the recession in our countries.

In <u>Assignment 2</u>, I will give information about Western Europe's economic situation, unemployment rate, number of immigrants, and increasing ethnic violence.

In <u>Assignment 3</u>, I will discuss several factors that contribute to the increasing ethnic violence in Western Europe. These factors include our weak economic situation, high unemployment, and increasing number of immigrants. I will also look at the immigrant situation and how they adapt to their new societies. The last factor I will discuss is the fast-growing anti-immigrant and neo-Nazi groups.

WORKING BIBLIOGRAPHY

"A Fall to Freedom: The Immigrant's Lot Is Not an Easy One." *World Press Review* Nov. 1989: 13.

"Closed Doors and Minds." *New Statesman & Society* 26 May 1989: 5.

Cooper, B., and D. Chasin. "Searching for a New Germany." *Journal of Commerce and Commercial* 16 April 1991: 8.

Coultan, M. "West Germans Fear for Their Comfort; Muted Welcome for the Newcomers." *World Press Review* Jan. 1990: 16.

"Is Europe's Boat Full?" *The Economist* 17 Aug. 1991: 41–42.

Kinzer, S. "A Wave of Attacks on Foreigners Stir Shock in Germany." *New York Times* 1 Oct. 1991: A1.

Loescher, G. "The European Community and Refugees." *International Affairs* Autumn 1989: 617.

Marks, J. "New Germany's Old Fears." *U.S. News & World Report* 14 Oct. 1991: 20.

"Racism Revived." *The Economist* 19 May 1990: 14.

For Assignment 2: Writing to Inform

THE INCREASING ETHNIC VIOLENCE IN WESTERN EUROPE

Ragnhild Olsen

In Germany there were more than 1,000 serious racist attacks in a recent year and most of them were against refugee hostels. Many people were killed and hundreds were injured (Bateman "Back to" 12–14). Not only Germany, but other Western European countries such as Britain, Spain, France, Italy, Belgium, Austria, Poland, Sweden, Norway and Denmark have also experienced this new wave of racial violence (Bateman "Back to" 14).

The number of refugees, mainly illegal immigrants, has increased rapidly within the last few years (Bateman "Tide of" 16). With the collapse of Communism in Eastern Europe (Lawday et al. 46–50) and unemployment soaring in North Africa, Western European countries are expecting millions more immigrants ("Europe's Elusive" 3). Despite the large number of immigrants, they cannot be blamed for the increasing ethnic violence we are now facing in Western Europe. We need to look at our countries' economic situations, our governments' immigration policies and the fast-growing anti-immigrant groups.

Western Europe's economic situation may be one reason for the increased ethnic violence. Our countries have experienced the highest unemployment rate since World War II (Church 16–17), and under these conditions racial violence often grows. The immigrants are blamed for taking away European jobs, even though this in reality very rarely happens (Church 16–17). In the European Community, the cost of handling applications for asylum is $5 billion each year ("Europe's Elusive" 3). This is a lot of money under the difficult economic circumstances European countries are experiencing now. However, Western Europe has an aging population due to a low birth rate (Lawday et al. 46–50), and our economy and societies will need the help of "young, hard-working and talented immigrants" (Bateman "Tide of" 16).

The economic situation in Western Europe may create the conditions for ethnic violence, but our governments' immigration policies have made these conditions possible (Bateman "Back to" 12–14). Immigration control has been a difficult problem for our democratic governments to tackle (Bateman "Tide of" 16) and has made it too easy to emigrate to our countries. So far, Germany has taken most of the immigrants, not only because of its wealth, but also because of liberal asylum laws (Lawday et al. 46–50). Our governments' procedures for handling asylum applications will probably fall apart unless something radically changes. Some have started, however, with more strict immigration rules such as tighter borders, checks on identity and employment and faster return of asylum-seekers (Bateman "Tide of" 16). The European Community countries are also trying to take a common stand on immigration. Britain has already decided to send back "economic" asylum-seekers and wants the other European Community members to do the same. The German government, in order to decrease the number of immigrants, is to pay the 2 million ethnic Germans remaining in Russia to stay where they are (Lawday et al. 46–50).

Ethnic violence has increased so rapidly because of the fast-growing anti-immigrant groups in Western Europe. In Germany there are now around 40,000 neo-Nazi activists (Bateman "Back to" 12–14). It looks like "nostalgia" for Nazism, and they seem to have forgotten that democracy is better than what we had before (Breslau 34). The extreme right-wing parties in all Western European countries are growing rapidly. In France, for example, Jean-Marie Le Pen, with his racist campaign, received up to 15% of the vote in opinion polls (Lawday et al. 46–50). According to federal police in Germany, right-wing extremists now commit more crimes each month than they did before in a whole year. Despite this, the response from the government is weak and the police tend to look the other way when neo-Nazis and other anti-immigration groups attack foreign people (Breslau 34).

There are no easy solutions to the increasing ethnic violence in Western Europe. Maybe, as a result of a rising economy and more effective immigration policies, the anti-immigration groups will lose influence and the "rise of racism" itself can be halted (Bateman "Back to" 12–14).

WORKS CITED

Bateman, Paul. "Back to the Future." *New Statesman & Society* 22 Nov. 1991: 12–14.

———. "Tide of Crisis." *New Statesman & Society* 12 Dec. 1991: 16.

Breslau, Karen. "When Neo-Nazis Run Free." *Newsweek* 29 July 1991: 34.

Church, George J. "Surge to the Right." *Time* 13 Jan. 1992: 16–17.

"Europe's Elusive Haven." *Maclean's* 4 Feb. 1991: 3.

Lawday, David, John Marks, Alexander Stille, Douglas Stanglin, and Jennifer Fisher. "No Immigrants Need Apply." *U.S. News & World Report* 9 Dec. 1991: 46–50.

For Assignment 3: Writing to Persuade

THE REASONS FOR THE INCREASING ETHNIC VIOLENCE IN WESTERN EUROPE

Ragnhild Olsen

In Germany there were more than 1,000 serious racist attacks in a recent year, and most of them were against refugee hostels. Many people were killed and hundreds were injured. Not only Germany, but other Western European countries such as Britain, Spain, France, Italy, Belgium, Austria, Poland, Sweden, Norway and Denmark have also experienced this new wave of racial violence (Bateman "Back to" 12–14). The violence may be due to the rapid increase in the number of refugees, mainly illegal immigrants, in the last two or three years (Bateman "Tide of" 16). With the Communist collapse in Eastern Europe (Lawday et al. 46–50) and unemployment soaring in North Africa, Western European countries are expecting millions more immigrants ("Europe's Elusive" 3).

Since the population of Western Europe consists not only of Western Europeans, but also of people from Eastern Europe, North Africa and Asia (Lawday et al. 46–50), the combination of different cultures, traditions, religions and languages sometimes leads to conflicts between immigrants and Western Europeans. However, I believe that the large number of immigrants and cultural differences is not the main reason for the increasing ethnic violence we are now facing in Western Europe. Rather, in my opinion, our countries' economic situations, our governments' immigration policies, and the fast-growing anti-immigration groups in Western Europe are to blame.

Western Europe's economic situation may be one of the reasons for the increased ethnic violence. Some claim, however, that there would not have been ethnic violence if all immigrants were white. This may be true, but I believe the ethnic violence in Western Europe is not caused by different skin color. It has been hard for Western European countries to adjust to such large numbers of immigrants over a short period of time, especially when the economies have been growing slowly and the unemployment rate is high. Western Europeans also blame their governments for using too much tax money on immigrants. This is understandable, when we know that in the European Community, the cost of handling applications for asylum is $5 billion each year ("Europe's Elusive" 3), which is a lot of money under the difficult economic circumstances these countries are now experiencing. All over Western Europe, politicians are working together to establish barriers against the expected flood of immigrants. However, immigrants can bring great benefits such as "energy, enterprise, fresh blood, and (usually) youth" ("The Would-Be" 14–15). This can be important when we know that Western Europe has an aging population due to a low birth rate (Lawday et al. 46–50) and that our economy and societies will need the help from "young, hard-working and talented immigrants" (Bateman "Tide of" 16) in the future.

While the economic situation in Western Europe may create the conditions for ethnic violence, I believe our governments' immigration policies have made these conditions possible (Bateman "Back to" 12–14). Each year hundreds of thousands of people come to Europe claiming to be political refugees. These seek asylum under the 1951 United Nations Convention on the Status of Refugees, which all members of the European Community have accepted. This forces Western European countries to take in anyone with a "well-founded fear of being persecuted for reason of race, religion, nationality, membership of a particular group or political opinion" ("Is Europe's" 41–42). The number of political asylum-seekers increased from 70,000 in 1983 to over 500,000 in 1990. During the 1950s and 1960s most political asylum-seekers came from Eastern Europe, whereas since the 1970s they have mostly come from the third world countries ("Is Europe's" 41–42).

With all the changes in Eastern Europe, we are expecting a lot more immigrants from those countries in the future. Immigration control has been a difficult problem for Western European democratic governments to tackle (Bateman "Tide of" 16), especially in differentiating between economic and political refugees. As the number of asylum-seekers has grown, the proportion given asylum has fallen ("Is Europe's" 41–42), and as Table 1 shows, the percentage of refugees accepted in 1991 is very low compared to the many refugees who applied (Post 36–38).

TABLE 1: *Immigration Statistics for Five Western European Countries, 1991*

	Immigrants Accepted under Regular Immigration Procedures	Refugees Applying for Asylum	Refugees Accepted
France	100,000[a]	27,262[b]	20%
U.K.	50,000[a]	34,000[b]	25%
Germany	230,000[a]	203,321[a]	5%
Austria	?	24,388[a]	13%
Italy	32,000[a]	25,762[b]	23%

[a] Estimated.
[b] Through June 1991.
? Information not available.
Source: David Lawday, John Marks, Alexander Stille, Douglas Stanglin, and Jennifer Fisher, "No Immigrants Need Apply," *U.S. News & World Report* 9 Dec. 1991: 46–50.

Table 1 also shows that the number of immigrants accepted in 1991 under regular immigration procedures was highest in Germany. Germany accepted most of the immigrants not only because of its wealth, but also because of its liberal asylum laws (Lawday et al. 46–50).

Western European governments' procedures for handling asylum applications will probably fall apart if radical changes are not made. Some have already started with stricter immigration rules such as tighter borders, checks on identity and employment, and faster return of rejected asylum-seekers (Bateman "Tide of" 16). However, in most Western European countries the processing of asylum applications is too slow. In countries where asylum-seekers get permission to work while they are waiting for a response to their asylum application, many are already well integrated by the time the decision comes. As a result, one third of those whose applications are rejected are allowed to stay. To avoid this, France, for example, gives applicants a small monthly allowance instead of work permits, and has reduced the processing to a few months ("Is Europe's" 41–42). European countries are also trying to take a common stand on immigration. Britain has already decided to send back economic asylum-seekers and wants the other European Community members to do the same. The German government plans to decrease the number of immigrants by paying the 2 million ethnic Germans remaining in Russia to stay there (Lawday et al. 46–50). So far, Italy has taken the most dramatic step by sending home most of the 45,000 Albanians who fled on overcrowded ships (Phillips 23–24).

Ethnic violence may have increased so rapidly because of the fast-growing anti-immigrant groups in Western Europe. Western European governments seem to play down this problem and do not recognize these groups' influence. However, it is important to face the growing number of anti-immigrant groups as a problem. For example, in Germany, there are now 40,000 neo-Nazi activists (Bateman "Back to" 12–14). There are also extreme right-wing parties in all Western European countries which are growing rapidly. In France, for example, Jean-Marie Le Pen, with his racist campaign, received up to 15% of the vote in opinion polls (Lawday et al. 46–50). Even in tolerant Denmark, attacks on foreigners are increasing, and opinion polls suggest that half of all Danes blame immigrants for unemployment and housing shortages ("Racism's Back" 15–16). According to federal police in Germany, right-wing extremists now commit more crimes each month than they did earlier in a whole year. Despite this, the response from the German government is weak and the police tend to look the other way when neo-Nazis and other anti-immigrant groups attack foreigners (Breslau 34). In addition, a recent opinion poll showed that 38% of West Germans said they had "sympathy" with the aims of the far right-wing groups (Bateman "Back to" 12–14).

There are no easy solutions to increasing ethnic violence in Western Europe. I don't believe the answer is to stop all immigration because Western European societies will need more people in the future; also, it is important to help genuine asylum-seekers, not only political refugees, but also those who run from poverty. However, it may be important to set a limit for immigration so that the Western European countries are better capable of integrating the ones who are accepted. I also believe that with a rising economy and more effective immigration policies, the anti-immigration groups will lose influence and the "rise of racism" itself can be halted (Bateman "Back to" 12–14).

WORKS CITED

Bateman, Paul. "Back to the Future." *New Statesman & Society* 22 Nov. 1991: 12–14.

——. "Tide of Crisis." *New Statesman & Society* 12 Dec. 1991: 16.

Breslau, Karen. "When Neo-Nazis Run Free." *Newsweek* 29 July 1991: 34.

"Europe's Elusive Haven." *Maclean's* 4 Feb. 1991: 3.

"Is Europe's Boat Full?" *The Economist* 17 Aug. 1991: 41–42.

Lawday, David, John Marks, Alexander Stille, Douglas Stanglin, and Jennifer Fisher. "No Immigrants Need Apply." *U.S. News & World Report* 9 Dec. 1991: 46–50.

Phillips, Andrew. "The Great Escape." *Maclean's* 4 Sept. 1991: 23–24.

Post, Tom. "A Fortress Mentality." *Newsweek* 9 Dec. 1991: 36–38.

"Racism's Back." *The Economist* 16 Nov. 1991: 15–16.

"The Would-Be Europeans." *The Economist* 4 Aug. 1990: 14–15.

Study Questions for Ragnhild Olsen's Portfolio

1. What is the thesis statement of Olsen's first assignment?

2. How has Olsen used her personal experience to develop her thesis in Assignment 1?

3. What differences do you notice between Assignments 1 and 2?

4. How do Assignments 2 and 3 differ? How are they similar? Identify places in Olsen's third assignment where she has integrated material from Assignments 1 and 2.

5. Are there questions in Olsen's papers that you wish she had answered?

6. What do you like about Olsen's portfolio?

7. What suggestions could you make to Olsen so that her papers would be better?

CHAPTER 6

Writing from Experience

This chapter introduces you to the first assignment in the writing portfolio, in which you will express the knowledge and opinions you have on your research subject. This chapter also includes explanations of the purpose and audience for this assignment and the methods of development you can use. The chapter concludes with directions for Assignment 1, related readings, peer review and self-evaluation forms, and the first draft and final version of a student paper.

As you know, *Writing from Sources* builds on the skills you have acquired in previous writing courses by progressing from personal, expressive writing to writing that is typical of academic work. In personal writing, which is the most common type of writing done in many introductory composition courses, you usually describe places, people, or events from the past. For instance, you may describe and narrate your journey to the United States, the most important day in your life, or a memorable person from the past.

In Assignment 1, you should use your skills in personal writing to build a foundation for the academic writing that comes later in the course. This assignment requires you to select a subject from the list in Chapter 5 and to relate your experience on that topic to the reader. The assignment will ask you to reflect on the topic, helping you to understand it better and prepare you for later assignments.

The readings included in this chapter will show you how some students have responded to this assignment. For example, when writing about Third World children, Ela Pastora Almendares Lopez reflects on their situation in her own country, Honduras. In her paper titled "Anti-Semitism in 20th Century Russia," Lyudmila S. Samsonova describes the history of anti-Semitism in her country. In the third paper, "Nuclear Issues: The Tragic Legacy of the Soviet Empire," Vladislav Skotar discusses the nuclear problems created as a result of the Soviet Union's collapse. Finally, Ponh Lanh, in an emotional paper titled "Surviving in Cambodia," explains how he survived the harsh Communist rule in Cambodia in the late 1970s.

PURPOSE AND AUDIENCE

How do people write about their experiences? Given below are summaries of two papers, which show you how the writers developed the research topics they had selected by describing and narrating their personal experiences. The summaries show how the writers adjusted their writing in order to make their topics clear to their readers.

A student from Sri Lanka writes on hunger in Third World countries. He notes that one of the main reasons for hunger is overpopulation, caused mainly by people who respect traditional values too much to practice birth control. In addition to overpopulation, the student notes that outdated agricultural methods also cause hunger. Since his readers may not be familiar with Sri Lanka, the focus of his paper, the student provides examples of traditional Sri Lankan values and agricultural methods.

A student from Norway writes on ethnic violence. She states that violent incidents between Norwegians and immigrants have increased rapidly in the past few years. Noting that many of her readers may already be aware of the cultural, religious, and language differences between the two groups, the student focuses on three other causes that may not be familiar to her readers: inefficient immigration laws, economic hardship and high unemployment in Norway, and the immigrants' reluctance to integrate into Norwegian society. To illustrate the third cause, she narrates an incident she saw in a television program, in which an Indian boy's parents did not allow him to interact with Norwegian children.

METHODS OF DEVELOPMENT

You may have chosen a particular research subject, such as ethnic violence or AIDS, because it has been in the news recently or because it may be affecting your country. As a result of your reading and television viewing, you may have a considerable amount of background information on the subject. However, unless you develop this information in a coherent manner, your readers may not fully understand it.

In the section on purpose and audience just discussed, you saw how two students developed their topics by using examples from their own countries. Now you will learn two methods of development that are important for writing from experience: the use of examples to illustrate your ideas; and the use of description and narration, which are very similar.

Using Examples

The easiest way to develop an idea is to provide examples. Sometimes an example can be a single word. For instance, an example of an Arab country would be Algeria. Alabama would be an example of a southern state in the United States. Examples help to develop generalizations and thereby develop an idea. For example, if you generalized that air pollution is harmful to health, you could provide examples of air pollutants such as carbon monoxide, sulfur dioxide, and lead, which are released to the atmosphere by industries and automobiles. You could then cite brain damage and lung disease as examples of the potential harmful effects of air pollutants.

Writers often use transitions to introduce their examples. Two of the most common transitions are "For instance" and "For example." These transitions signal to us that the writer is going to develop an idea with the use of examples.

In personal, expressive writing, such as in Assignment 1, the examples may come from your personal experiences. However, in more academic writing, such as in Assignments 2 and 3, you will use facts and statistics gathered from library research to develop your ideas.

Description and Narration

A useful addition to some types of writing is description of personal experience. This description can be of a place, a person, an object, or even a series of events. When the description is about events, such as a story, we say that the writer is using **narration.**

Usually, description is based on a writer's own experience, as in the papers by Ela Pastora Almendares Lopez and Ponh Lanh included later in this chapter. It is also possible for the description to be partly or totally from the writer's imagination, as in works of fiction. A writer may also retell someone else's experience, as Almendares does in relating the story of poor parents seeking medical help for their child.

Whether based on firsthand or secondhand experience, and whether real or imaginary, good descriptive writing gives the reader a clear picture of the person, place, or event being described. The writer uses details and precise word choices to make the writing vivid. A careful choice of nouns and verbs gives the reader an accurate mental picture.

Nouns and Verbs

Building a large vocabulary of nouns and verbs is particularly helpful for ESL students; careful word choices make speech and writing clearer, more precise, and more interesting. The best way to expand your vocabulary is to read, listen to, and use English at every opportunity. Take special note of the interesting new words you hear, especially the nouns and the verbs. Use context clues or a dictionary to understand the meaning of these new words. Figure 6.1 illustrates how you can use concrete, specific nouns to show the reader exactly what you are describing.

As Figure 6.2 shows, you can also add **adjectives** to make your nouns more specific and concrete. Notice how the substitution of specific nouns for vague, general ones and the addition of adjectives can make a sentence more vivid:

Original:

After our exercise, the food was good.

Revised:

After our hard run, the cold, sweet orange refreshed us.

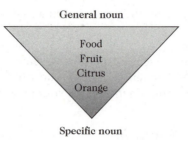

General noun

Food
Fruit
Citrus
Orange

Specific noun

FIGURE 6.1 *From General to Specific Nouns*

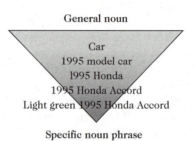

General noun

Car
1995 model car
1995 Honda
1995 Honda Accord
Light green 1995 Honda Accord

Specific noun phrase

FIGURE 6.2 *Using Adjectives to Make Nouns Specific and Concrete*

EXERCISE 6.1   **USING SPECIFIC WORDS**

Construct charts such as the ones shown in Figures 6.1 and 6.2 that give more specific words for the following general terms. Then write descriptive sentences using your specific terms.

animal	problem
vehicle	tool
person	plant

The revised sentence shown earlier also uses a descriptive, active **verb** *refreshed* rather than the colorless verb *was*. In fact, the heart of any effective sentence is its verb, especially when the verb describes an action that readers can picture. As Figure 6.3 shows on page 97, we can move from weak, general verbs to verbs that are more concrete and descriptive. Notice how the following sentence is improved by a more precise choice of nouns and verbs and the use of adjectives:

Original:

The animal moved across the space.

Revised:

The old bear lumbered across the sunny field.

Concrete, specific nouns and verbs can help bring a picture into the reader's mind.

Adverbs and descriptive phrases can also add to the power of sentences:

The old bear lumbered awkwardly across the hot field in search of cool water.

Descriptive details make writing both clear and more interesting to read.

✓ While carefully chosen **modifiers** (adverbs and adjectives) can improve descriptive writing, it's possible to use too many of them. Sentences with too many modifiers may sound amateurish:

The big, round, orange moon appeared slowly and grandly over the tops of the tall, black, majestic pine trees in this peaceful little clearing.

Strong nouns and verbs make writing more effective than the use of too many modifiers.

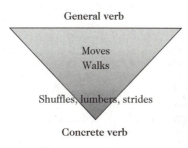

General verb

Moves
Walks

Shuffles, lumbers, strides

Concrete verb

FIGURE 6.3 *From General to Concrete Verbs*

WRITING DESCRIPTIVE SENTENCES   **EXERCISE 6.2**

Revise the following sentences so that they will bring a picture to the minds of your readers. Use specific nouns and verbs. You can also use modifiers to complete your descriptions, but be careful not to overuse them. You may expand the description to a passage longer than one sentence.

(continued)

(continued)

1. The truck moved down the road.
2. A person was in front of the building.
3. Adding a weak acid changed the color of the solution.
4. Due to the weather, the flight was delayed.
5. Research indicates that ESL students from non-English-speaking countries experience more culture shock.

Sensory Description

Most descriptive writing depends on visual details—what the writer has seen and wants the readers to visualize in their minds. However, it is also possible to use descriptive details using the other four senses.

The following list contains descriptive words for each of the five senses. Note that some of the words are more specific than others.

Sight	*Sound*	*Smell*	*Touch*	*Taste*
light	noise	musty	soft	salty
glare	bang	fresh	velvety	sweet
moonlight	tinkle	rainwashed	sharp	sour

EXERCISE 6.3   USING SENSORY WORDS

Add at least three words to each column in the preceding list of sensory words. Make your words as specific as possible. Then write sentences that include the sensory words you have added.

Writing to Create an Effect

Often the main purpose of descriptive writing is to inform the readers about something. For example, an engineer may describe a machine so that readers will have a clear picture of what the machine looks like and perhaps how it works. At other times, however, writers use descriptive writing to create an effect—to evoke a mood for their readers or to influence their opinions about what is being described. When you read the paper by Almendares Lopez in this chapter, you will see that she uses description to create a mood of sadness, and perhaps to influence her readers' opinions about the plight of poor children in Third World countries.

DESCRIBING A PLACE   **EXERCISE 6.4**

Describe a place that you enjoy. If possible, visit this place and take notes so that you will describe it accurately. You may also describe a favorite place from memory. In your description, choose words that will create a vivid mental picture for your readers.

WRITING A BRIEF NARRATIVE   **EXERCISE 6.5**

Write a brief narrative (about 100–200 words) on one of the following topics. This narrative may be real or imaginary.

an exciting time	a scary time
a happy time	a sad time

DESCRIBING AN OBJECT   **EXERCISE 6.6**

Describe one of the following objects so that the reader will be able to picture it accurately. Your purpose for this exercise is to inform, not to create an effect.

  a room in your apartment, house, or dorm

  a tool that you know how to use

  your car, motorcycle, or bicycle

  the outside of a building on this campus

LEARNING NOUNS AND VERBS   **EXERCISE 6.7**

From your readings in *Time* or *Newsweek* each week, make a list of at least five new nouns and five new verbs. Your list should contain the word, the original sentence from *Time* or *Newsweek,* and a brief definition.

ASSIGNMENT 1: EXPRESSING KNOWLEDGE AND OPINIONS

This paper will reflect the writing skills you have learned in this chapter.

First, select a research topic from the list in Chapter 5.

In Assignment 1, express your knowledge and opinions on the topic you have chosen. Since the paper is based on your knowledge and opinions, you should not refer to any sources in the library or elsewhere. Make sure that you write a clear thesis statement and a topic sentence for each paragraph. Ensure proper organization, transitions, and cohesion.

In Assignment 2, you will provide more information on the topic you have chosen. In Assignment 3, you will argue your position on the topic. Both of these assignments are based on library research.

Your papers should be typed or computer-written. The paper for Assignment 1 should be about 500 words (two double-spaced pages) in length. For all three assignments your readers will be your classmates. Your instructor will tell you when your first draft and final version are due. (Please submit your first draft with the final version.)

READINGS

To help you write Assignment 1, we have included papers from four students. As you read these papers, note how the writers have used thesis statements to express their main ideas and how they have used examples, description, and narration to develop their ideas. The study questions at the end of each paper will guide you in group discussions.

THIRD WORLD CHILDREN

Ela Pastora Almendares Lopez

Third world countries have many problems that industrialized countries have learned to solve a long time ago. One of these problems is the early death of many infants. In my country, Honduras, many children in the rural areas die before reaching one year of age. This is due to three basic situations that plague the poor, uneducated society of my country.

First of all, to have a big family in the rural areas is a tradition. This shows that God wants to bless this family by giving them many offspring. But many mothers in the rural areas do not have the ability to take care of all their children at the same time. The first baby for these mothers is an especially hard experience, since no one tells them how to take care of the baby. For example, when my mother got married at the age of seventeen years, she did not how to take care of a baby. During that time, having a baby for her was like playing with a doll. She did not know how to bathe, dry, and feed a baby, or what to do if the baby got sick. Because of her inexperience, my first brother died of bronchitis, a disease that is not fatal if you take care of it in time.

In addition to the lack of experience in taking care of children, the lack of medical treatment and basic medicine also creates problems. In many rural areas, there are no medical centers; therefore, the people have to walk many miles to get some help. It is sad when these distressed parents arrive at the nearest medical center too late to save the life of their child. For instance, my cousin, a medical student, related to us many sad experiences about rural people who come to the city looking for medical treatment to save their children. Once, he met a couple from Yaguasire, a distant town, who were desperate because their child had terrible diarrhea and vomiting. Due to malnutrition and his other diseases, their three-year old child looked to be much younger. This couple told my cousin that the nurse in their little town just gave them aspirin as medicine because it was the only thing that she had. After two weeks of intensive care, the baby survived.

The last situation is that in my country the political and military budgets are more important than medical care. My country has spent a huge amount of money each year on military equipment, instead of using this money to establish some good rural medical centers. It is very expensive to provide these centers with medical personnel, adequate equipment, and medicines to save these children. Even though there are a lot of medical personnel available to work in rural areas, the government has said that it does not have the money to pay the salaries of these people. It is ironic when the government gives large amounts of money to incumbent politicians to pay for expensive political campaigns and has very little money left for medical care.

In conclusion, many rural children will die each year due to the inexperience of their mothers and the lack of medicines and medical equipment. I hope that in the future the government makes the necessary changes to save the rural children, since the children of today are the future of tomorrow.

Study Questions for Ela Pastora Almendares Lopez's Paper

1. How does Almendares Lopez introduce the paper? Did she get your attention at the beginning?
2. What is her thesis statement?
3. How is the thesis developed?
4. Is the description based on firsthand experience?
5. Does Almendares include her opinions in the paper?
6. Can you find three specific nouns and verbs?
7. What is the overall effect the paper had on you?

ANTI-SEMITISM IN 20TH CENTURY RUSSIA

Lyudmila S. Samsonova

For many centuries, the ethnic groups that constituted Russia were living in peace. During the 20th century, the existing situation changed significantly. With the change of the political system, the problem of anti-semitism arose. Jews were the most persecuted people for more than forty years. In my opinion, the Socialist Revolution of 1917 and the Stalin period

(1924–1954) were mainly responsible for anti-Semitism in Russia, which continues to date.

Anti-semitism began in Russia with the communist system at the beginning of the twentieth century. The main idea of the Socialist Revolution of 1917 was to abolish the rich, the aristocracy, and to establish the power of the workers. At that time, the majority of well-educated, upper-class people were Jews. As a result, the slogan "kill the rich" became synonymous with "kill the Jews." Therefore, upper- and middle-class Jewish people were persecuted, exiled, shot, or jailed. There was not a family that did not experience the loss of relatives or other atrocities. My great grandfather, a famous lawyer, was imprisoned for twenty-five years and worked as a carpenter in a concentration camp. All of his brother's family were shot. His sister and her husband, both public prosecutors, were lucky enough to be only banished to Siberia and not killed by the KGB.

During the "Stalin period" of 1924–1954, ideological and political pressure against the Jews continued, but the reasons for discrimination were different. After the revolution, the economic situation changed for the worse. Communist leaders had to find scapegoats who could be blamed for the failure of the new socialist system. Because the Jewish people were the most victimized, they were thought by the Communist party to be the most hostile group. Stalin established the new slogan "find an enemy and kill him." Jewish people were then pursued and punished for no reason as enemies. For example, when a young woman, a member of the Communist party, was found suffocated in the Public Park, the KGB arrested her Jewish friend, Abram Rodkevich, and accused him of murder without any investigation. Two weeks after he was shot, the stepfather of the murdered woman made a confession to the police. Very often Jews were accused of political crimes as well. As the new history books reveal, Stalin was obsessed with the idea that some leaders of the Communist party planned to overthrow him. On his order, famous leaders such as Trotsky, Kirov, and others who were gaining in popularity among the people were executed. In the "Doctor's Case," a group of Jewish doctors were charged with anticommunist activities which had the destruction of the socialist republic and the extermination of the communist leaders as its goal. Those doctors were tortured by the KGB and forced to make false confessions, and then were sentenced to death.

Political repression and discrimination against Jews did not stop when Stalin's power ended. The idea of anti-Semitism, so deeply embedded in the minds of ordinary people, has continued since then. The Jews were blamed for all the hardships in Russia. They were not welcome to the universities, and teachers were often more strict with them than with other students. Also, Jews had problems finding a job. The Jews who wanted to have a career had to change their last name, so it would not sound Jewish. Garry Kasparov, world chess champion, changed his last name in order to have a career as a chess player. Even at schools, children with Jewish names could be oppressed. I remember my high school class. We had just one Jewish girl, Sarah, who was a normal, vivid child with big expressive eyes and a sincere smile. Nothing distinguished her from others except her last name, Zinhelmeyer. The others kids gossiped and joked about her all the time. One day we had to act Shakespeare's "Romeo and Juliet," and Sarah fitted the image of Juliet. The teacher chose her for the main role but the other girls started to scream and yell. Sarah tried to control herself, but eventually, with tears in her eyes, she asked: "What is wrong with me?" Definitely, there was nothing wrong with her; something was wrong with us. I will never forget those words and the lesson she taught me.

Belonging to a certain ethnic group should not be a reason for hatred or maltreatment. In the 20th century, the new political system played a major role in the discrimination against Jews, but the Soviet people were the ones who readily believed in the inferiority, the hostility, and the guilt of the Jewish people. I think that in order to stop the ethnic violence in Russia and to find solutions for its economic and political problems, Russian people need to understand that it was not the Jews who caused all the problems.

Study Questions for Lyudmila S. Samsonova's Paper

1. How does Samsonova introduce the paper? Did she get your attention at the beginning?
2. What is her thesis statement?
3. How is the thesis developed?
4. Is the description based on firsthand experience?
5. Does Samsonova include her opinions in the paper?
6. Can you find three specific nouns and verbs?
7. What is the overall effect the paper had on you?

NUCLEAR ISSUES: THE TRAGIC LEGACY OF THE SOVIET EMPIRE

Vladislav Skotar

Before the collapse of the USSR in December 1991, the nuclear arsenal of the country was located in three republics—Ukraine, Kazakhstan and Russia. The arsenal has always been under unified command (the "button" could be activated only under mutual consent of the President, the Defense Minister, and the Chairman of the Joint Chiefs of Staff). The Atomic Energy Ministry was the sole executive body in charge of all civil nuclear facilities. Each and every procedure involving a minimal amount of radioactive materials was strictly monitored and controlled.

After the break-up of the Soviet Union the whole system of centralized control fell apart. As a result, the legacy of the Soviet nuclear arsenal has become a great concern of the international community. Specifically, this concern centers on nuclear weapons in the former republics of the USSR, nuclear plants and reactors, brain drain, and proliferation of radioactive materials.

Shortly after the Belovezhskaya Push'cha Agreement officially declared that the Soviet Union had ceased to exist, President Yeltsin requested that all nuclear weapons should be relocated from the former republics to Russia. The reason for this demand was that the Russian leadership feared the republics playing the "nuclear card" in order to blackmail Russia. That was especially dangerous because of Russia's dispute with Ukraine over the fate of the Black Sea Fleet and the Crimean Peninsula. Moscow even used economic pressure, stopping gas and oil supplies to Kiev (the capital of Ukraine), in order to make Ukraine comply with those demands. Although the president of Ukraine agreed to those demands, the process of political bargaining over the withdrawal is still in progress.

The problem facing Kazakhstan, the second Republic in possession of nuclear arms, is of a different origin. Since the end of World War II this large Asian republic has been the biggest nuclear testing site in the Soviet Union. The huge arid locality near the town of Semipalatinsk is studded with the remains of multitudes of nuclear devices. People who lived there were deliberately deceived by the Soviet government, which repeatedly proclaimed nuclear tests to be harmless to humans, provided that the necessary safety measures were taken. The problem was that those measures were not taken. One of my school teachers, a retired colonel, told me about numerous war exercises held in Kazakhstan in the 1950s, when actual nuclear bombs were exploded and the soldiers who participated in those military exercises were not even told that nukes were used. Although he said that there had been no radiation-inflicted injuries, I read numerous stories about people suffering from the consequences of taking part in or being witnesses to such tests.

The harbinger of the problem of civil nuclear power use was, of course, the Chernobyl tragedy. The nuclear accident affected millions of Ukrainians and Belorussians. Thousands of acres of fertile soil were contaminated. Thousands of people were forced to flee for their lives. Those who stayed are bound to die soon of radiation disease. The worst thing is that there are more than half a dozen reactors of the same type throughout the Commonwealth of Independent States. Besides, some of those reactors are located in politically unstable regions, for example, in Armenia, which currently is in a state of war with neighboring Azerbaijan. That, of course, increases the probability of an accident no less tragic than Chernobyl. Any act of terrorism will lead to disastrous consequences, which may have an impact on millions of lives.

The nuclear problem also has several international aspects. A very serious matter that concerns the world is brain drain. Economic difficulties forced many Russian physicists and nuclear engineers to leave their jobs in search of better-paid work in foreign countries. This poses a potential threat to global security, for such nations as North Korea, India, Pakistan,

Israel and Iraq strive to or have already obtained nuclear weapons. There are chances that the new employer of those Russians would be, say, a dictator bent on nuclear war.

In addition, after World War II, the Soviet Union assisted a number of nations, such as Poland, North Korea and China, in building their own nuclear power plants. Those countries used to export nuclear wastes for disposal to the Soviet Union and, in return, purchase the necessary radioactive fuel (enriched plutonium). Now, as concerns over nuclear safety grow in Russia, it is more and more reluctant to be either a radioactive materials producer or a nuclear graveyard.

Nuclear safety in the former republics of the USSR draws the intent attention of the international community. I am deeply convinced that a solution to the problems I outlined could be reached only by joint forces of all the parties involved. I strongly advocate the idea that the United Nations in general, and the International Atomic Energy Agency in particular, should dedicate more effort to promoting responsibility among the world's governments as far as nuclear safety is concerned. I do believe that if we manage to resolve the nuclear problems in my country, the world will be assured of a better future.

Study Questions for Vladislav Skotar's Paper

1. What is the thesis of Skotar's paper?
2. How does he use personal experiences to develop his thesis?
3. Does Skotar express his opinions in this paper?
4. What did you like about this paper?
5. Imagine Skotar is a student in your class. What suggestions would you give him so that he could improve his paper?

SURVIVING IN CAMBODIA

Ponh Lanh

The Civil War in my country, Cambodia, ended in 1975. At that time, I was nine years old. From 1975 till 1979, I lived under Communist rule. Within these four years, many children around my age died of starvation. As for me, I survived through the entire four years by knowing how to lie and how to steal.

Lying is not a good thing to do, but at that time I had to lie to save my life and my brother's life. At one time, my brother Thivin and I went into a banana farm to steal bananas. We were looking for good bananas and we finally found some. It was a big and tall banana tree with big and ripe banana fruits. My brother and I took turns trying to climb that banana tree, but it was impossible. The banana tree was slippery, just like walking on ice with tennis shoes on. My shorts and legs got wet trying to climb that banana tree. My brother's clothes got wet too. So after many unsuccessful attempts, we gave up climbing and tried to cut the tree down. As we were peeling off its dead bark so that we could cut it down easily, an adult farm guard came at us. He had a big long knife in his hands and he was walking towards us very fast. We were scared. My brother was about to run away, but I grabbed his hand. Before I could say something to Thivin, that guard was right in front of us. He asked us what we were doing to his banana tree. My brother was scared and shaking and couldn't say anything. So I spoke for both of us. I told him that we were lost and we were looking for some moss on the tree so that we could find our direction again. In Cambodia, many farmers believe that moss grows on oak trees from the north side. If someone gets lost in the woods, he could go and look for moss on the oak tree, which would show him the north direction. After I told the guard we were lost and looking for some moss, he said that moss doesn't grow on banana trees; it grows on oak trees. Then he asked what direction we wanted to go. I told him we wanted to go east. He showed us which direction was east. We said "thank you" and got out of that farm as fast as we could. So by telling a lie, my brother and I got away without any harm.

Besides lying, stealing is also not a good thing to do. However, I had to steal to keep myself from starvation. Many children around my age stole fruits and vegetables just like me, but I never got caught. At one time, I stole a baby pig. It was very difficult to steal compared to fruits and vegetables because a baby pig can cry. Anybody within a twenty-yard radius can hear a baby pig crying. So I went to the pig farm, which was located at one section of the camp, after the pigs' keeper fed them. It was around six in the evening. Many pigs were screaming as they were fighting for food. Pretending to urinate, I stepped on one of the baby pigs. It was kind of dark when I stepped on that pig. Nobody could tell whether a pig was screaming because it was fighting for food or because I was stepping on it. After I killed the pig, I left it there. Later that night, I went back to get the pig and went deep into the wood. I cooked that pig and ate it all by myself. On my way back to camp, I stopped by a pond to wash my hands and mouth well. I chewed leaves and spat them out a couple of times. I also rubbed leaves on my hands. That way when I got back to the camp, nobody could tell that I had eaten meat. Stealing was not a good and easy thing to do, but I had to steal to keep myself from starvation.

Many people died during that four years of living under the Communist rule. These people died of starvation and from not knowing how to talk their way out of a bad situation. As for me, I survived because I knew how to lie and how to steal.

Study Questions for Ponh Lanh's Paper

1. What is the thesis of Lanh's paper?
2. How does he develop his thesis?

3. Did you enjoy Lanh's paper? Why or why not?
4. Can you think of ways Lanh could improve his paper?

PLANNING/SELF-EVALUATION OF DRAFT

In Chapter 2, we discussed the importance of choosing and narrowing a topic, analyzing the purpose of your paper, and analyzing your readers. In order to help you plan your paper, we have included a Planning/Self-Evaluation of Draft form. (See page 108.) As you fill out this form, you will think carefully about your paper. Your responses on the form will show you how your paper is going to be organized. The form can also be used to self-evaluate your draft before your classmates peer-review it. Items 10, 11, 12, and 13 on the form are mainly for your self-evaluation.

PLANNING/SELF-EVALUATION OF DRAFT

1. Topic

2. Tentative title

3. My purpose—Describe:

                  Persuade:

4. My readers know/do not know this topic well.

5. By reading this paper, my readers will think about . . .

6. My thesis statement is:

7. My topic sentences are:

    1.

    2.

    3.

    4.

8. I have arranged the topic sentences in this order because . . .

9. The examples to support my topic sentences are:

    Topic sentence 1:

    Topic sentence 2:

    Topic sentence 3:

    Topic sentence 4:

10. I need to develop the following points/paragraphs:

11. I need to omit the section on _____ because . . .

12. My opening is interesting because . . .

13. My closing is effective because . . .

PEER REVIEW

You have many readers in this class. Your primary reader, of course, is your instructor, who will also grade your writing. But your papers will be read by your classmates as well, and during the peer-review process, they will have a chance to comment on your writing. By giving comments and suggestions on your classmates' papers, and receiving them on your own papers, you will be able to revise and improve your papers.

To guide you in the peer-review process, we have provided peer-review sheets at the end of this chapter and Chapters 8 and 9. Follow the instructions carefully. Write your comments and suggestions after reading your classmate's paper two or three times. Always offer specific comments and suggestions. For instance, instead of saying "Some of your sentences are confusing," you could write "The second sentence in your third paragraph is not clear. You should define *hyperinflation* and give an example." In addition to writing these suggestions on the peer-review sheet, you may write additional comments and questions directly on the writer's paper.

When you have completed the peer review, go to the student whose paper you reviewed and further explain your comments and suggestions to him or her. Use the peer-review sheet on page 110 to guide you in this discussion. Ask the writer questions; questions about their writing motivate writers to think critically.

ASSIGNMENT 1—PEER REVIEW

Author:

Reviewed by:

First, read the paper straight through to get a quick, general impression. On the second or third reading, respond to the paper according to the guidelines given below. Please offer specific comments. After writing your responses, discuss the paper with the writer. Thank you.

1. Did you enjoy the paper? (Yes or no). Why, or why not? Please be specific.

2. Is the thesis statement clear? (Yes or no). If not, how can the thesis be clarified?

3. What is the topic sentence of the second paragraph?

    Do all the sentences in the paragraph relate to the topic sentence? (Yes or no). If not, how can the writer improve the paragraph?

4. What is the topic sentence of the third paragraph?

    Do all the sentences in the paragraph relate to the topic sentence? (Yes or no). If not, how can the writer improve the paragraph?

5. Write five transitions (transitional words or phrases, repetition of key words or phrases, use of synonyms) you found in the paper.

    Does the paper need additional transitions? (Yes or no). If yes, where?

6. Find two places where the writer has used specific examples to develop an idea.

    Specify another place where you think an example is needed.

7. Is there any place in the paper where you were confused? (Yes or no). If so, draw wavy lines under the confusing parts, and explain why you were confused.

8. What are the strong points of the paper?

9. How can the paper be improved?

REVISION

The following paper, "Third World Children" by Jit-Meng Wong, will show you how a student revised the first draft of his paper based on the comments and suggestions he received from a classmate. The first draft and the final version of the paper are included along with the peer review Wong received from a classmate and the outline he wrote based on the peer reviewer's comments and suggestions.

THIRD WORLD CHILDREN

Jit-Meng Wong

In today's worlds, perhaps you and I live in a healthy life while many children in the third world countries, such as Vietnam and Ethiopia, suffer disease and malnutrition. Daily newspapers such as *USA Today* or in monthly magazines such as *Time* supply different kinds of articles that concern these issues. They also illustrate how some third world children live a poor, diseased life. Even today, thousands of children die because of inefficiency and unproductivity in their country's economy and natural disasters such as floods, earthquakes and others. In theory, these will yield many different kinds of diseases that will be damaging to the children. In my assumption, these problems can be solved with a satisfactory settlement. I think there are three adequate ways to aid those children.

First, the Union of World Nation and the local governments must be responsible to solve all kinds of problems. As we know, the figures of the death of the children are increasing every month though the governments provide many necessities to the children. So, perhaps other reasons cause the deaths of these children. For instance, in Ethiopia, children use water for drinking and bathing from the river where the animals also bathe. Can you imagine how dirty that water is? This water surely carry all kinds of diseases to the children. In addition, many children live in small and dirty shacks where they do not receive fresh air. In such conditions, the Union and the government must immediately take some action to solve this dilemma. They can provide a clean water from other sources such as wells. Besides that, they can construct clean living places for poor families. If these steps are taken, many children can be saved quickly.

The media from the rich countries, such as the United States, Germany and Japan, can provide their advanced and sophisticated technological devices in media to help those children. As we know, not everybody in this world know what is occurring presently in many third world countries. Consequently, the media are accountable for defining and telling the world the real problems. The media can use these advanced devices in many different ways. For instances, the media can provide documentation concerning the situation and the problems that are happening in those third world countries. The media also can tell the world that the children need food and medication now.

Finally, the wealthy people donate their money and others provide their time to help those children. They can contribute their funds through the performance or public events where they would effortlessly get more funds from the whole world. Those children need a lot of help to lead healthy lives. If they have everything they need, they would live a better life and be happy as the other children in this world.

In conclusion, we must give our sympathy and help to save those children. Although there are three ways to help those children that I mentioned above, we still need more supports to solve these problems quickly. If everybody shows his or her support, I think everything can be solved easily and the children will live a happy and healthy life.

Here is Sachiko Kawabata's review of Jit-Meng Wong's paper. Note how specific her comments and suggestions are.

ASSIGNMENT 1—PEER REVIEW

Author: *Jit-Meng Wong*

Reviewed by: *Sachiko Kawabata*

1. Did you enjoy the paper? (Yes or no). Why, or why not? Please be specific.

    I enjoyed parts of your paper. There were many spelling and grammar mistakes. The paragraphs were not well organized so I found it difficult to read.

2. Is the thesis statement clear? (Yes or no). If not, how can the thesis be clarified?

    Your thesis statement is not clear. Is it in the last sentence of the first paragraph?

3. What is the topic sentence of the second paragraph?

    "The Union of World Nation and local governments must be responsible to solve all kinds of problems."

    Do all the sentences in the paragraph relate to the topic sentence? (Yes or no). If not, how can the writer improve the paragraph?

    The paragraph is confusing. What is the Union of World Nation? Is it the United Nations? You can improve the paragraph by deleting the second sentence.

4. What is the topic sentence of the third paragraph?

    "The media from rich countries . . . can provide them advanced and sophisticated technological devices in media to help the children."

    Do all the sentences in the paragraph relate to the topic sentence? (Yes or no). If not, how can the writer improve the paragraph?

    Yes, all the sentences relate to the topic. But what do you mean by "advanced and sophisticated technological devices"? Also, to whom should these devices be provided? And for what purpose?

5. Write five transitions (transitional words or phrases, repetition of key words or phrases, use of synonyms) you found in the paper.

    also. However, First, For instance, In addition

(continued)

(continued)

6. Find two places where the writer has used specific examples to develop an idea.

    First paragraph: Vietnam and Ethiopia are given as examples of third world countries. Third paragraph: The United States, Germany, and Japan are examples of rich countries.

    Specify another place where you think an example is needed.

    Examples of advanced and sophisticated technological devices.

7. Is there any place in the paper where you were confused? Draw wavy lines under the confusing parts, and explain why you were confused.

    Your thesis is not clear. The fourth paragraph is confusing. I couldn't understand it.

8. What are the strong points of the paper?

    Many transitions and some examples are used.

9. How can the paper be improved?

    Write an outline of your paper. You will then see the paper's problems. Paragraph 4 is confusing. Revise or delete it. The paper has many grammatical mistakes. You should visit the writing lab.

Following Kawabata's advice, Wong wrote this outline of his paper:

THIRD WORLD CHILDREN OUTLINE

Thesis: Thousands of children died because of inefficiency and unproductivity in their country's economy and natural disasters. . . . There are three adequate ways to help these children.

Paragraph 1 Topic: The Union of World Nations and the local government must be responsible to solve all kinds of problems.
> Examples: unclean water in Ethiopia
> bad housing

Paragraph 2 Topic: The media from rich countries can provide . . . devices to help these children.
> Examples: of devices: none
> uses: can provide documentation of the situation and problems

Paragraph 3 Topic: Wealthy people donate their money . . . to help those children.
> Examples: performance and public events

After writing the outline, Wong agreed with Kawabata's comments and suggestions. He then visited the writing lab twice and also met with his instructor. The final revision of Wong's paper follows.

IMPROVING THE LIVES OF THIRD WORLD CHILDREN   *title*

Jit-Meng Wong

Many of us live in a happy and healthy society. We can be considered lucky *lead-in* when compared with children in some Third World countries such as Vietnam and Ethiopia. Newspapers such as *USA Today* and the *New York Times* and magazines such as *The Economist* and *Newsweek* often contain articles which concern Third World children. Even today, thousands of these *thesis* children die because of disease and malnutrition. In my opinion, these children can be saved in three ways.

First, the Third World governments and the United Nations must take *topic sentence* a more active role. Although the governments provide food and medicine to their children, the rate of malnutrition and disease is still very high. Perhaps the most serious problems should be solved first. For instance, in *example* Ethiopia, some children drink from the same sources that animals use. In addition, many children live in small, dirty, and crowded places which are harmful to their health. So, the governments with the help of the United Nations should provide clean water and better housing for the children. If these problems can be solved, many children may live a healthier life.

topic sentence

Rich countries, such as the United States, Germany, and Japan, can provide sophisticated equipment such as televisions and video cameras to Third World countries. This equipment can be used to teach people of Third World countries how to lead healthier lives. Since many of these people are illiterate, they cannot read, so newspapers and posters may be useless. But anyone can understand pictures, so televisions set up in village centers

example

could be used to educate people. This is done successfully in India. The media from rich countries can also help by providing more news stories about the children. Such stories will arouse the concerns of foreign governments to increase their help to Third World children.

topic sentence

Finally, people in rich countries can donate their money to help the children in Third World countries. Already, many organizations like "Save the Children" and CARE collect money in rich countries to help children

examples

in the Third World. Concerts such as "Live Aid" where musicians perform free have collected much money for the poor in Third World countries.

conclusion

In conclusion, the world's future is in the hands of these children. If they are provided enough food and medicine, they will grow up to become happy and useful citizens. If not, they will only make the situation worse.

CHAPTER 7

Using and
Acknowledging Sources

Most of the writing you do in your courses and later in your career will be based on information obtained from sources other than from your own knowledge and experience. For the second assignment in this book, for example, you are asked to gather information from at least two sources, preferably newspaper or magazine articles. To locate these sources, you will visit the library, find newspaper and magazine articles on your topic, and then include relevant information in your paper. This chapter discusses how to locate and use this information in the papers you write for this and other courses.

USING THE LIBRARY

To find information for your papers, you will need to visit your school's library and perhaps other libraries as well, such as the public library. The sources you find in the library will enable you to write an informative paper for Assignment 2 and to support your arguments in Assignment 3.

One of the best investments in time you can make is to become familiar with your school's library. In fact, you may be able to attend an orientation class or take a tour conducted by a librarian to introduce students to the library's resources. Get to know the reference librarians who work with students; you may need their help to find library materials.

Libraries have materials of all kinds, including books, magazines, journals, audiovisual materials, and reference books. More than 40,000 books are published annually in the United States. When the thousands of magazines, journals, and newspapers are added to this number, we truly have an information explosion. Before the days of computers, library users consulted a card catalog to help them find materials they needed. Now, instead of card catalogs, most libraries have computer-based online catalogs, which can help you quickly identify the materials you need. In fact, the online catalogs of some libraries list the materials contained in other libraries as well so that if your library does not have the book or periodical, you could do a computer search to see if another library has it. Learn to use your library's online catalog as soon as possible. Through this catalog, you can locate books, periodicals (magazines and journals, also called "serials"), and other sources. To locate a specific article in a periodical, however, you will need to consult an index.

Indexes will help you identify all the sources that have been published on a topic within a certain time period. Indexes may cover a general combination of topics, such as the *Readers' Guide to Periodical Literature,* or they may be limited to a certain broad area, such as business or education. The *MLA Bibliography,* for example, indexes articles and books about literature. Indexes also come in a variety of forms: printed and bound like a book, on CD-ROM storage systems at computer terminals, or even online terminals that provide access to large, computerized databases. *InfoTrac,* a CD-ROM index that contains articles of general interest, is available in many libraries.

Visit your school library to see exactly what indexes are available to you, since they vary from school to school. You can learn to use these indexes from an orientation class or with the help of a reference librarian.

To use the library resources efficiently, it is helpful to know some of the specialized terminology that librarians use. Box 7.1 provides a glossary of terms to which you can refer when seeking the help of a librarian.

Searching for Books and Periodical Articles

Use the following guidelines when you search for books and periodical articles at the library.

Searching for Books

1. Go to a computer terminal that contains the library's online catalog.
2. If you have a particular book or an author in mind, search by the author's name first. An author can be a personal name, a corporation, an association, or the sponsor of a conference.
3. If you do not know the author's name or cannot find it, search by title.
4. If you want a book on a general subject, search by subject.
5. Write down the call number, check the book's location in the library, and get the book from the shelves.
6. If the book has been checked out, go to the circulation desk and ask for the book to be recalled.
7. If the library does not own the book, go to the reference desk and request the book through interlibrary loan service.

If you run into a problem or have any questions, get advice from a reference librarian.

Searching for Periodical Articles

1. If you need periodical articles on a specific subject, use periodical indexes. The most general periodical index is *Readers' Guide to Periodical Literature.* Specialized indexes, such as *General Science Index* or *Social Science Index,* list publications in specific fields.
2. Look under relevant subject headings in the index to find references to your topic, and write them down.

Glossary of Library Terms	**BOX 7.1**

Abstract	A summary that gives the important points of a book or an article.
Almanac	An annual publication that contains facts and statistics (e.g., *World Almanac*).
Bibliographic information	The information needed to locate an item in a library. For a book, it consists of author, title, place of publication, publisher, and date of publication.
Bibliography	(1) A list of books and articles used when writing an article or a book. In the MLA format, the bibliography is called Works Cited. In the APA format, it is called References. (2) A publication that contains only lists of books, articles, and other works on a topic. A bibliography can be useful in locating information on a topic.
Bound periodical	Several issues of a journal or magazine that are fastened together between hard covers into a single volume.
Call number	The number given to each item in the library. An item can be located by its call number.
CD-ROM	Compact Disk-Read Only Memory. These disks hold thousands of pages of information. *InfoTrac* is on CD-ROM.
Circulation desk	The counter where you check out, return, and renew books. The circulation desk is usually near the entrance to the library.
Database	An electronic collection of information. Many databases, such as *Info-Trac*, are on CD-ROM.
Encyclopedia	A book containing information on every subject (e.g., *World Book*) or limited to a specialized subject (e.g., *International Encyclopedia of Social Sciences*).
Index	(1) A list of subjects discussed in a book. (2) A list of journal articles arranged by subject and/or author (e.g., *InfoTrac, Readers' Guide to Periodical Literature*). Some indexes are in the form of books. Others may be accessed by computer.
Interlibrary loan (ILL)	Borrowing a book or getting a copy of an article from another library. This service may be free to students.
Journal	A periodical that contains scholarly articles written by experts in a subject area (e.g., *Journal of Reading, TESOL Quarterly*).
Magazine	A periodical meant for the general public rather than for scholars (e.g., *Newsweek, Time*).
Microform	Books or articles on film instead of paper. A roll of film is called *microfilm;* a sheet of film is called *microfiche*. Microform must be read on special machines.

(continued)

(continued)

Overdue	This means a book has not been returned on the due date.
Periodical	A publication issued regularly (e.g., newspaper, magazine, journal).
Primary source	Original material (e.g., letters, scientific papers, news accounts, poems, short stories, novels).
Recall	The way by which you request a book that has been checked out by another person.
Reference book	A book you can consult for specific facts and background (e.g., *World Almanac*). You may not need to read the entire book.
Reference desk	A place where librarians give you directions, answer questions, and show you how to find and use materials. The reference desk is located near the shelves containing encyclopedias, dictionaries, indexes, and statistical sources.
Reserve	A collection of books and journal articles set aside by professors for use by students in their classes. The reserve material is usually kept behind the circulation desk.
Secondary source	Material at least one step removed from the originals (e.g., book reviews, literary criticism, histories).
Serial	Publications that appear at regular intervals (e.g., newspapers, magazines, journals, annual reports, annual reviews).
Volume	Individual issues of a periodical bound together into a single book. Large books are also divided into volumes.

3. If you know the title of the periodical, you need not go to the periodical index. You can check directly on the online catalog to see if the library has the periodical.

4. Go to the shelves and get the periodical. Periodicals cannot be checked out of the library, so you may have to take notes from the article or make photocopies.

5. If the library does not own the periodical, go to the reference desk and request the article through interlibrary loan service.

If you run into a problem or have any questions, get advice from a reference librarian.

✓ To succeed in the American educational system, you must learn to use the library. When using the library, you will often need the help of a reference librarian, whose job is to show you the bibliographies, indexes, abstracts, and other reference sources that the library owns and to help you in using them. Reference librarians will suggest the best sources for your research topic and will help you in obtaining materials on interlibrary loan.

Get to know your reference librarians well. And remember to take your course syllabus and writing assignments when you seek help.

SUMMARY, PARAPHRASE, AND QUOTATION

When you use information from other sources to support and strengthen your ideas, you should smoothly blend others' writing with your own. There are three ways to include information from other writers in your writing assignments. You can (1) summarize, (2) paraphrase, or (3) quote directly from other writers. Each time you summarize, paraphrase, or quote directly, you must tell the reader where you got the information. This acknowledgment is called **documentation.**

Generally, quotation is considered the easiest; paraphrase is difficult, and summary is the most difficult. Summary and paraphrase allow you to use your own words. However, summary is shorter than paraphrase; therefore, you should summarize the most, then paraphrase, and quote the least.

Summary

A **summary** is a shorter version of the original source. Only the important points of the source are included in a summary; most details and supporting examples are left out.

How to Summarize

You may find it easy to read a passage, reflect on its main ideas, and summarize these ideas in your own words. However, if you find that difficult, here's a process you can use to summarize:

1. Read the passage carefully.
2. Underline the main ideas; they may be found in the thesis statement and topic sentences. Delete most details and examples.
3. Rewrite the main ideas in complete sentences.
4. Substitute synonyms for words in the original. Rearrange words and sentences to make the writing your own.

✓ If you cannot think of a synonym, try guessing the meaning of a word in context. For example:

After meeting a person for the first time, we often retain a *gestalt* of that person but cannot remember specific details like eye color.

When they found jobs, many single mothers became financially *solvent* and no longer needed welfare.

Can you guess the meaning of the italicized words? Check your guess by looking up these terms in the dictionary.

5. Shorten the passage by combining sentences.

6. Remember to identify the original source in parentheses after the summary or to name the source in the introduction of your summary. You will also give full bibliographic citation of this source in your Works Cited (see page 136).

The following examples, taken from student writing, will show how this process can work.

EXAMPLE A

Original Source

When Singapore, a 236-square-mile island, gained independence in 1965, it was faced with a major pollution problem caused by motor vehicles, the widespread smoking habit, and littering. To control this problem, the Singapore government imposed high taxes on vehicle ownership, imposed excise taxes on tobacco, and enforced strict anti-littering laws. Because of the cleaner environment resulting from these policies, many multinational companies have invested in Singapore (Boon Hwee Ng 3).

1. Underline main ideas; delete most details and examples. When <u>Singapore</u>, a 236-square-mile island, gained <u>independence</u> in 1965, it was faced with a <u>major pollution</u> problem <u>caused by motor vehicles</u>, the widespread <u>smoking</u> habit, and <u>littering</u>. To control this problem, the Singapore government <u>imposed high taxes on vehicle ownership</u>, imposed <u>excise taxes on tobacco</u>, and enforced <u>strict anti-littering laws</u>. Because of the <u>cleaner environment resulting</u> from these policies, <u>many multinational companies have invested in Singapore</u> (Ng 3).
(The main ideas underlined are: Singapore/independence/major pollution/ caused by motor vehicles, smoking, and littering / imposed high taxes on vehicle ownership, excise taxes on tobacco, strict anti-littering laws/cleaner environment resulting/many multinational companies have invested in Singapore.)

2. Rewrite main ideas in complete sentences. At independence, Singapore had a major pollution problem caused by motor vehicles, smoking, and littering. High taxes on motor vehicles and tobacco and anti-littering laws resulted in a cleaner environment. As a result, many multinational companies have invested in Singapore.
(Although the sentences are different from those in the original, this passage still has many words from the original.)

3. Substitute synonyms; rearrange words and sentences. Since independence, high taxes on vehicles and tobacco and strict anti-littering laws have eliminated pollution in Singapore. The cleaner surroundings have attracted many multinational companies to that country.
(Substitutions: at = since; resulted in a cleaner environment = eliminated pollution; invested in = attracted; Singapore = that country
Sentence combination: eliminates the repetition of motor vehicles, smoking, and anti-littering laws)

Summary

Since independence, high taxes on vehicles and tobacco and strict anti-littering laws have eliminated pollution in Singapore. The cleaner surroundings have attracted many multinational companies to that country (Ng 3).

EXAMPLE B

Original Source

The 1980s were called the "lost decade" of Latin America. During this period, the standard of living in the region declined rapidly. Many Latin American countries suffered from extremely high inflation. For example, by 1987, the inflation rate in Bolivia had gone up to 20,000 percent a year. This gloomy picture prompted many economists to argue that the Latin American economy in the 1990s would be worse (Ligia Machado 1).

1. Underline main ideas; delete most details and examples. The 1980s were called the "lost decade" of Latin America. During this period, the standard of living in the region declined rapidly. Many Latin American countries suffered from extremely high inflation. For example, by 1987, the inflation rate in Bolivia had gone up to 20,000 percent a year. This gloomy picture prompted many economists to argue that the Latin American economy in the 1990s would be worse (Machado 1).
(The main ideas underlined are: 1980s/Latin America/standard of living/ declined rapidly/high inflation/1987/inflation rate in Bolivia/20,000 percent a year/prompted many economists to argue/Latin American economy/ 1990s/worse.)

2. Rewrite main ideas in complete sentences. In the 1980s, in Latin America, the standard of living declined rapidly. Many countries suffered from high inflation. For example, by 1987, the inflation rate in Bolivia was 20,000 percent a year. This prompted many economists to argue that the Latin American economy in the 1990s would be worse.
(Although the sentences are different from those in the original, this passage still has many words from the original.)

3. Substitute synonyms; rearrange words and sentences. In the 1980s, the standard of living in Latin America fell quickly. Many countries were

badly affected by high inflation. By 1987, the annual inflation rate in Bolivia, for example, was 20,000 percent. Consequently, many economists predicted that the economy would decline further in the 1990s.
(Substitutions: declined rapidly = fell quickly; suffered = badly affected; a year = annual; this prompted = as a result; argued = predicted
Rearranged words: In the 1980s, in Latin America, the standard of living declined rapidly/In the 1980s, the standard of living in Latin America fell quickly; the inflation rate in Bolivia was 20,000 percent a year/the annual inflation rate in Bolivia was 20,000 percent)

Summary

In the 1980s, the standard of living in Latin America fell quickly. Many countries were badly affected by high inflation. For example, by 1987, the annual inflation rate in Bolivia was 20,000 percent. Consequently, many economists predicted that the 1990s would be worse (Machado 1).

You can summarize a passage of any length—a sentence, a paragraph, or even an entire book or article.

Features of a Summary

When you summarize a source, your summary must meet the following criteria:

The summary must be shorter than the original.

The summary must have the same meaning as the original. Retain the main ideas in the original source and leave out most details and examples. Never add information that is not in the original.

The summary must always include a reference to the original source.

EXERCISE 7.1   SUMMARIZING PASSAGES

Summarize the following passages using the six steps on pages 123–24.

A. When Mikhail Gorbachev came to power in 1985, few people could have imagined that such an event would bring about the collapse of a superpower, the Soviet Union. For decades, the Communist Party was the center of Soviet life. After the failed coup of August 1991, the party disappeared overnight, its leadership disbanded, its offices were padlocked, and its publications were silenced. The Soviet Union officially came apart when all its fifteen republics declared themselves independent. These events have left the United States as the only economic, political, and military superpower (Syed Khan 5).

B. Many people believe that the U.S. economy has already declined because the U.S. has a big deficit and has become the largest debtor nation in the world. However, the U.S. is still very powerful both economically and politically. It is true that Japanese companies are spreading all over the world and Japanese products are sold worldwide. But many more American companies, such as GM, Ford, and Motorola, are selling their products worldwide. *Fortune* magazine announces the world's biggest companies each year. In 1990, the company with top sales was GM; and Exxon and Ford Motors came in third and fourth. The only Japanese company to make the top ten, Toyota, came in sixth place (Takao Suzuki 7).

SUMMARIZING A PAPER   EXERCISE 7.2

Summarize the following paper by Tetsuya Okita.

HUMAN FACTORS: A MAJOR CAUSE OF FAMINE

Tetsuya Okita

According to recent research, the number of famines does not appear to decrease with the advance of technology. Most people believe that famines are caused by droughts or floods, factors beyond human control. But they are wrong. Droughts and floods cause famines when coupled with human-assisted disasters. I believe that a major cause of famine is human factors such as civil wars and government mismanagement.

First, civil wars can cause famines. Take a country like the Sudan, which experienced drought for a few years. When the civil war broke out, millions of Sudanese died of starvation. This is because the United Nations (UN) and other food suppliers were cut off by the war. For example, the Red Cross suspended all flights to Sudan because all the landing strips in areas held by the Sudan Peoples' Liberation Army (SPLA) had been bombed by the government (Prendergast 32). However, in Botswana, which faced a ten-year drought in the 1980s ("The Horn" 38), nobody died of starvation, mainly because the country did not have a civil war. Relief food could be transported easily by road or by air.

Secondly, government mismanagement can be a major cause of famine. For example, Ethiopia could actually feed itself, since more than half of the country's arable land is being cultivated. But in 1988, the government sold nearly all the grain reserves to earn foreign exchange for weapons purchases (Prendergast 32). As a result, millions of Ethiopians died in the famine which lasted from 1989 to 1991. On the other hand, in the mid-1980s, although Kenya faced a drought as severe as the one that led to

(continued)

(continued)

Ethiopia's great famine, it only faced local food shortages ("The Horn" 38). This is because the Kenyan government had acknowledged the problem early and imported enough grain to feed its people.

In conclusion, famines can be caused by civil wars and government mismanagement. Good and competent governments can reduce the number of famines and save people's lives. I believe that world hunger will be reduced only if rulers want to stop avoidable human-assisted disasters.

WORKS CITED

"Bad Gets Worse." *The Economist* 9 Nov. 1991: 46.

Prendergast, John. "The Crisis of Survival." *Africa Report* Jan.–Feb. 1991: 31–33.

"The Horn Is Empty." *The Economist* 11 May 1991: 37–38.

Paraphrase

A **paraphrase** contains all the information in the original source written in your own words. Details and supporting examples must be included; no part of the original is left out.

How to Paraphrase

1. Read the passage carefully.

2. Substitute synonyms and rearrange words and sentences to make the writing your own.

3. Break up long sentences; combine short sentences.

4. Make sure that the resulting paraphrase is worded very differently from the original, yet means the same thing as the original sentence. No more than three consecutive words in the paraphrase can be identical to the original.

5. Either name the original source in parentheses after the paraphrase or identify the source in the introduction of your paraphrase. In your list of Works Cited, give full bibliographic information on the source. (See "Acknowledging Sources" on page 136.)

✓ If you have successful experience with paraphrasing, you may not find it necessary to go through all of these steps. But, if you are still learning this important skill, this process may help you, as the following examples will show.

EXAMPLE A

Original Source

When Singapore, a 236-square-mile island, gained independence in 1965, it was faced with a major pollution problem caused by motor vehicles, the widespread smoking habit, and littering. To control this problem, the Singapore government imposed high taxes on vehicle ownership, imposed excise taxes on tobacco, and enforced strict anti-littering laws. Because of the cleaner environment resulting from these policies, many multinational companies have invested in Singapore (Boon Hwee Ng 3).

1. **Substitute synonyms and rearrange words.** At independence in 1965, Singapore, a 236-square-mile island, was heavily polluted as a result of motor vehicles, a popular smoking habit, and littering. The Singapore government began to tax owners of motor vehicles and tobacco, and enacted anti-littering laws to solve this problem. These policies resulted in cleaner surroundings, and, as a result, Singapore has attracted many multinational corporations.

2. **Break up long sentences; combine short sentences.** At independence in 1965, Singapore, a 236-square-mile island, was heavily polluted. Motor vehicles, a popular smoking habit, and littering were the causes. To reduce pollution, owners of motor vehicles, and tobacco, were taxed by the Singaporean government. It also enacted anti-littering laws. These policies resulted in cleaner surroundings. As a result, Singapore has attracted many multinational corporations.

Paraphrase

At independence in 1965, Singapore, a 236-square-mile island, was heavily polluted. Motor vehicles, a popular smoking habit, and littering were the causes. To reduce pollution, owners of motor vehicles, and tobacco, were taxed by the Singaporean government. It also enacted anti-littering laws. These policies resulted in cleaner surroundings. As a result, Singapore has attracted many multinational corporations (Ng 3).

EXAMPLE B

Original Source

The 1980s were called the "lost decade" of Latin America. During this period, the standard of living in the region declined rapidly. Many Latin American countries suffered from extremely high inflation. For example, by 1987, the inflation rate in Bolivia had gone up to 20,000 percent a year. This gloomy picture prompted many economists to argue that the Latin American economy in the 1990s would be worse (Ligia Machado 1).

1. Substitute synonyms and rearrange words. In Latin America, the 1980s were called the "lost decade." The living standard of Latin Americans fell rapidly during the decade. A very high rate of inflation was seen in many countries such as Bolivia, where it had risen to 20,000 percent by 1987. As a result, many economists predicted that the economy of Latin America would get worse in the 1990s.

2. Break up long sentences; combine short sentences. In Latin America, the 1980s were called the "lost decade." The living standard of Latin Americans fell rapidly during the decade. A very high rate of inflation was seen in many countries. The inflation rate in Bolivia, for instance, had risen to 20,000 percent by 1987. As a result, many economists predicted that the economy of Latin America would get worse in the 1990s.

Paraphrase

In Latin America, the 1980s were called the "lost decade." The living standard of Latin Americans fell rapidly during the decade. A very high rate of inflation was seen in many countries. The inflation rate in Bolivia, for instance, had risen to 20,000 percent by 1987. As a result, many economists predicted that the economy of Latin America would get worse in the 1990s (Machado 1).

Features of a Paraphrase

When you paraphrase a source, your paraphrase must meet the following criteria:

The paraphrase must have exactly the same meaning as the original.

The paraphrase must be different enough from the original to be considered your own writing. No more than three consecutive words can be the same as the original.

The paraphrase must always include a reference to the original source.

EXERCISE 7.3   PARAPHRASING PASSAGES

Paraphrase the following passages using the five steps on page 128.

A. Each day, the average American produces about 4 pounds of trash, or approximately more than half a ton of trash each year. As a nation, more than 179 million tons of trash are produced annually. According to the Environmental Protection Agency (EPA), this staggering volume of refuse is projected to increase by 20 percent, that is, to 216 million tons, by the year 2000. Today, there is much debate on the best method to solve the trash problem: incinerate or recycle? (Boon Hwee Sim 5)

B. Cyprus was well known in antiquity for its abundant natural resources, especially copper mines and forests. Its wealth made it attractive to the great powers in the eastern Mediterranean. The Assyrians, the Egyptians, and the Persians conquered it in turn. Despite Cyprus' multicultural history, the Greeks, who were the first to establish city-states in the second millennium BC, managed to preserve their culture. Around the middle of the 19th century, Cyprus came under Turkish rule. The Turks ruled till the end of the century, when the island was ceded to Britain. By the end of the Turkish rule, Turks who did not wish to return to their homeland had established a minority group in Cyprus (Pavlos Louca 2).

C. In 1989, the World Health Organization's immunization program prevented the deaths of 2.2 million children. Moreover, the percentage of immunized children rose from 5 percent in 1974 to over 60 percent in 1989. However, although 2.2 million were saved in one year, another 3 million children under the age of five died due to preventable diseases. In fact, in developing countries, 40,000 children die each day due to malnutrition and disease (José Quino-Gonzalez 2).

✓ Why should you paraphrase when it's easier and more accurate to quote? First, paraphrase ensures that you have understood what is said in the original source. Second, your purpose in using the paraphrase could be different from that of the writer. For example, Quino-Gonzalez's purpose in passage C is to argue that, despite the efforts of the World Health Organization (WHO), many children die of malnutrition and disease. However, you could use the statistics to show that the WHO has carried out a successful immunization program and saved the lives of 2.2 million children.

So paraphrase is preferred to direct quotation. In fact, many instructors have limitations on the amount of quotations they will accept in a paper, perhaps 10 to 15 percent of the total. Nevertheless, quotations can be quite effective if used appropriately in a paper. The following section gives guidance on the use of direct quotations.

Direct Quotation

Direct quotations are the words of another person as they appeared in the original source. Why and when should you quote? First, a summary or paraphrase may rob the original writing of its impact. For instance, it's better to quote the following speech by Great Britain's wartime Prime

Minister Winston Churchill. A summary or paraphrase would not have the rhythm and beauty of Churchill's words.

> We shall fight on the beaches, we shall fight on the landing ground, we shall fight in the fields and the streets, we shall fight in the hills; we shall never surrender.

Quoting will also help you to support your claims with direct evidence from an authority. Moreover, by quoting, you acknowledge a writer's expertise in a certain subject. Using the exact words of an expert adds weight to your argument.

However, don't quote too much; as already noted, not more than 10 to 15 percent of your paper should be quotations. Students sometimes quote whole paragraphs unnecessarily, as seen in this example:

> Even though prostitution is illegal, foreign women continue to arrive in Japan to earn a living as prostitutes. Between the months of May and June 1992,
>
> > 84 people were diagnosed with AIDS and 36 of these were Thai prostitutes in their twenties. The data indicates that foreign prostitutes represent a large percentage of the infected people in Japan. Tokyo, Ibaraki, and Nagano ranked as the cities with the highest number of people with AIDS and the largest number of foreign prostitutes. ("AIDS Increase" 12)

Although the preceding information is important to the student's paper, the sentences need not be repeated exactly. Instead, this information should be paraphrased.

HOW TO USE DIRECT QUOTATIONS

1. Copy the quotation exactly, including the punctuation and capitalization of the original.

2. If the quoted material is less than five typed lines, enclose the quotation between double quotation marks. This is called *in-line quotation*. For example:

   > The *MLA Handbook for Writers of Research Papers* defines *plagiarism* as "the act of using another person's writing without acknowledging the source" (20).

3. If the quotation is five or more typed lines, set the quotation off from the main body in the text. Indent the quotation 10 spaces from the left margin and double-space. Do not use quotation marks for *set-off quotations*. For example:

```
The Business Writer's Handbook defines standard English this way:
        There are two broad varieties of written English:
        standard and nonstandard. These varieties are
        determined through usage by those who write in the
        English language. Standard English is characterized
        by exacting standards of punctuation and
        capitalization, by accurate spelling, by exact
        diction, by an expressive vocabulary, and by
        knowledgeable usage choices. (Brusaw, Alfred, and
        Oliu 220)
```

4. If you want to leave out some words of the original quotation, use ellipses (three spaced periods) to show where the words are left out. However, make sure that you don't change the meaning of the original. For example:

   The Business Writer's Handbook defines standard English as "the language of business, industry, . . . education, and the professions" (Brusaw, Alfred, and Oliu 220).

5. If you want to insert your own words into a direct quotation or change the quotation, you can use brackets to show the words that are not part of the original. This may be necessary to make the sentence grammatically correct or to make the quotation clear to the reader. For example:

   Original:

   According to Jones, "It is a serious problem facing the nation" (35).

   Edited:

   According to Jones, "[Unemployment] is a serious problem facing the nation" (35).

6. Ensure that your quotation is in the same number (singular or plural), person, and tense as the sentences around it. If your sentences are in the present tense, the quotation should be in the present tense. For example, the following quote does not agree with the sentences around it.

   Most people believed that famines were beyond human control. According to Suzuki, "they are wrong." Famines can be caused by human-made disasters. (The first sentence is in the past tense; the quote is in the present tense.)

7. Always introduce direct quotations within your text by referring briefly to the author or the title of your source. It may also be a good idea to tell your readers why the source is important and give the author's credentials that establish her or him as an expert on the subject.

8. Use a full citation in your list of Works Cited section to show the source of your quotation. (These citations are discussed later in this chapter.)

EXERCISE 7.4   ANALYZING QUOTATIONS

Analyze the following quotations and answer the questions that follow them.

A. On May 28, 1992, the civilian chief of the UN Peacekeeping Force and his team arrived in Cambodia's capital, Phnom Penh. According to Philip Shenon, a United States journalist,

> On September 25, 1992, 2,000 Japanese soldiers arrived at Phnom Penh as part of the United Nations peacekeeping force. Most of these Japanese soldiers have been assigned to an engineering operation that will rebuild bridges and roads destroyed during Cambodia's 13-year civil war. (Shenon 10L)

1. Is the quotation in A. necessary?
2. What are the shortcomings of the quotation in A.?

B. According to the National Center for Atmospheric Research, as a result of the greenhouse effect, the Northern hemisphere will have an average increase of 1 or 2 degrees in temperature by the year 2000 (Sommers 120). In the words of Bill Mackibben, author of *The End of Nature,*

> the various processes that lead to the end of nature have been essentially beyond human thought. Only a few people knew that carbon dioxide would warm up the world, for instance, and they were for a long time unsuccessful in their efforts to alert the rest of us. Now it is not too late, as I shall come to explain, to ameliorate some of the changes and so perhaps avoid the most gruesome of their consequences. But scientists agree that we have already pumped enough gas into the air so that a significant rise in temperature and a subsequent shift in weather are inevitable. (67)

1. Is the quotation in B. necessary?
2. What are the shortcomings of the quotation in B.?

Before we conclude this section, here is a quick comparison of summary, paraphrase, and quotation.

Summary Versus Paraphrase

A *summary* focuses on the most important ideas in the original. It is a reduction of the original; minor points and details are left out.

A *paraphrase* contains all the information in the original. It is a translation of the original into your own words; nothing important is left out.

Original Sentence:

About 4,000 chain stores have formed frequent-shopper clubs that offer freebies and discounts to customers who sign up, based on how much they spend (McCarroll 49).

Summary:

Customers can join frequent-shopper organizations at many chain stores (McCarroll 49).

Paraphrase:

Frequent shoppers can join organizations formed to give them free and discounted items at 4,000 chain stores, depending on how much they spend (McCarroll 49).

Summary Versus Quotation

A *summary* is written in the writer's own words; it is also shorter than the original.

All the words in a *quotation* are identical to the words in the source. Therefore, it is also the same length as the source.

A *summary* or a *paraphrase* can contain brief quotations from the original work. However, if you include more than three consecutive words from the original, you must use quotation marks.

Original Sentence:

Women from ages 16 to 25 pay less for automobile insurance because they have fewer serious accidents, especially accidents involving driving while intoxicated, and their driving records, like those of women of all ages, are 23 percent better than those of men (Smith 68).

Summary with Quote:

Because women have fewer accidents and driving records that are "23 percent better than those of men," they pay less for car insurance (Smith 68).

ACKNOWLEDGING SOURCES

Each time you use a summary, paraphrase, or a direct quotation in your paper, you must tell the reader where you got the information. In other words, you must give credit to the original author for words or ideas that are not your own. Acknowledging the sources of your information is called documenting your sources. If you fail to provide this documentation, you will be guilty of plagiarism (literary theft).

Documentation of your sources is necessary whether you have summarized, paraphrased, or quoted directly from your source. There are two parts to the documentation procedure: parenthetical citations within the body of your paper and a list of Works Cited at the end of your paper.

Parenthetical Citations

The purpose of a **parenthetical citation** is to show the reader the source and page number of the material you are quoting, paraphrasing, or summarizing. The citation appears in your text immediately after the material you have borrowed.

The citation usually includes the author's last name and the page number(s) where you found the original material. The author's last name will help the reader find the complete reference in your list of Works Cited at the end of your paper. If the author's name is not given (an anonymous source), use a short version of the title of the book or article.

When you introduce borrowed material with a brief mention of your source, you don't need to repeat that information in the parenthetical citation that follows the borrowed material. Study the examples already given for direct quotations. You will notice that most of them have only page numbers in the parentheses after the borrowed material. For these quotations, the author's name or a short title of the source was used in the introduction.

Also note the punctuation for the in-line quotations. The parentheses are usually placed at the end of a sentence, before the period. For set-off quotations, the parentheses are placed after the period.

List of Works Cited

At the end of your paper, you will have a list of Works Cited that gives full bibliographic information for the sources you have used. These sources will be listed in alphabetical order.

Below are sample entries that might appear in a list of Works Cited. If a source you have used does not fit one of these examples, you can consult the *MLA Handbook for Writers of Research Papers* for additional help.

Book by a Single Author

Fairbanks, Carol. *Prairie Women: Images in American and Canadian*
    Fiction. New Haven: Yale UP, 1986.

Book by an Agency or a Corporation

American Medical Association. *The American Medical Association*
    Family Medical Guide. Rev. ed. New York: Random, 1987.

Book by More Than One Author

Berry, Jason, Jonathan Foose, and Tad Jones. *Up From the Cradle*
    of Jazz: New Orleans Music since World War II. Athens: U of
    Georgia P, 1986.

An Edition

Chaucer, Geoffrey. *The Works of Geoffrey Chaucer.* Ed. F. N.
    Robinson. 2nd ed. Boston: Houghton, 1957.

An Article from a Daily Newspaper

Lanier, Kim. "Mobile No Longer Wettest." *Mobile Register* 5 Feb.
    1995: 1A.

An Anonymous Article

"Drunkproofing Automobiles." *Time* 6 Apr. 1987: 37.

An Article from a Weekly or Biweekly Magazine

Walsh, John. "U.S.-Japan Study Aim Is Education Reform." *Science*
    16 Jan. 1987: 274-75.

An Article from a Monthly or Bimonthly Magazine

Frazer, Lance. "Yours, Mine, or Ours: Who Owns the Moon?" *Space*
    World Nov. 1986: 24-26.

An Article in a Scholarly Journal with Continuous Annual Pagination

Santley, Robert S. "The Political Economy of the Aztec Empire."
    Journal of Anthropological Research 41 (1985): 327-37.

(*Note:* The number just before the parenthetical year is the volume
number of the journal.)

An Article in a Scholarly Journal That Paginates Each Issue Separately

Winds, Robin W. "The Sinister Oriental Thriller: Fiction and
    the Asian Scene." *Journal of Popular Culture* 19.2 (1985):
    49-61.

(*Note:* The number 19.2 signifies volume 19, issue 2.)

An Editorial

```
Evans, Harold. "Free Speech and Free Air." Editorial. U.S. News &
        World Report 11 May 1987: 82.
```

An Interview

```
Jones, Anna. Personal Interview. 7 Jan. 1991.
```

Material from a Printed Source on CD-ROM

```
Somogyi, Stephan. "E-mail Gets Smart." MacUser 10 (1994): 32.
        Infotrac: Expanded Academic Index. CD-ROM. Information
        Access. March 1994.
```

Material on CD-ROM Only (No printed source)

```
Withington, William A. "Ho Chi Minh City." The Software Toolworks
        Illustrated Encyclopedia. CD-ROM. New York: Grolier
        Electronic Publishing. 1990.
```

Material from the Internet

```
de Soysa, Minoli. "Sri Lankan Government Must Avoid War, Analysts
        Say." SLNet 0639 (19 April 1995): n. pag. Online. Internet.
        20 April 1995.
```

EXERCISE 7.5   USING AND ACKNOWLEDGING SOURCES

1. What do we mean by "documenting our sources"?
2. When should we document our sources?
3. What is the difference between a direct quotation and a paraphrase?
4. When do we use in-line quotations?
5. When do we use set-off quotations?
6. When do we use ellipses?
7. How do we edit a direct quotation to make it clearer or grammatically correct?
8. In the paper by Teck-Ann Tan (in Chapter 9), find one example for each of the following:
   a. a parenthetical citation for a paraphrase

b. a parenthetical citation for a direct quotation
c. a quotation edited with brackets
d. the source for a table
e. a direct quotation that is introduced within the text
f. a direct quotation with ellipses

9. In the Works Cited page of Tan's paper, find the following:
   a. an entry with both an author and an editor
   b. a book
   c. a journal or magazine article

CHAPTER 8

Writing to Inform

This chapter continues the study of the research process, beginning with the second assignment in the writing portfolio. For this assignment, you will explore library sources to collect information on the research topic you have selected. This chapter also includes explanations of the purpose and audience for informative writing, the research proposal and working bibliography, the difference between facts and issues, and the methods of development for informative writing. The chapter concludes with Assignment 2, related readings, and peer-review forms.

In Assignment 1, you expressed your knowledge and opinions on the research topic you had selected. The assignment was the link between personal and academic writing, helping you to build a foundation for the academic writing that begins with Assignment 2.

The readings included in this chapter will show you how some students have responded to this assignment. In her paper "Meiji, Mother of Modern Japan," Nita Bavikati writes on a fact that is not well known outside Japan: The modernization of Japan began as far back as the nineteenth century, during the Meiji period. In the second paper, "Ethnic and Religious Violence in Nigeria," Michael K. Nsah discusses the situation in his country. In the third paper, "Women of the Veil: Happy or Oppressed?" Amir K. Shafi describes the situation of women in some Muslim countries. Next, Faisal Hussain discusses the spread of AIDS in Africa and Asia, revealing that nearly 70 percent of the people infected with AIDS in 1992 were in Africa. Finally, Syed Arafat Kabir, in "Women's Place in Islam," describes the role of women in the Muslim world. Although Kabir and Shafi wrote on the same topic and cited similar sources, you will see how their papers differ in approach and content.

PURPOSE AND AUDIENCE

When we write to inform, our purpose is to educate our readers about a topic of which we have some knowledge. Usually, informative writing is not based on our personal experience, but rather on published sources. Informative writing is the type of writing you will do most frequently in your university courses.

The examples that follow will show you how two writers developed informative papers by using and acknowledging sources, as well as by using the methods of development introduced later in this chapter. The examples will also show you how these writers adjusted their writing in order to make their topics clear to their readers.

1.   For publication in the *Reader's Digest,* a doctor writes an article on brain tumors. He begins by describing a tumor's appearance and then details how a brain tumor is diagnosed and the surgical procedures required for its removal. Knowing that his readers are not familiar with medical terminology, he carefully defines a number of terms. He classifies tumors into malignant and benign types, and states that nearly half the brain tumors diagnosed in the United States are benign. To support this statement, the doctor cites recent statistics and quotes a well-known neurosurgeon. He concludes by saying that areas of the brain once off-limits to surgery are now routinely accessible.

2.   For her freshman writing class, a student writes about air pollution and the alternative sources of energy that are available. First, she classifies these alternatives into geothermal, wind, solar, hydro, and biomass. She defines a number of terms, including biomass. She cites a number of sources in her paper and identifies these sources in a list of Works Cited.

RESEARCH PROPOSAL AND WORKING BIBLIOGRAPHY

Although Assignment 1 was based on your knowledge and opinions, the second and third assignments are based on library sources, such as periodicals and books. In Assignment 2, you will further describe your topic using these sources. In Assignment 3, you will first take a position on the topic and then argue in support of the position you have taken.

In order to prepare for Assignments 2 and 3, you will be asked to write a research proposal and a working bibliography. In the **research proposal,** you will state your point of view (the thesis) on your topic and explain how you plan to develop Assignments 2 and 3. Since these two assignments are based on library sources, you will be asked to attach a **working bibliography** of at least 10 sources to the research proposal. In Chapter 5, you saw the proposals written by Zhiling Liu and Ragnhild Olsen, and assignments that resulted from the proposals.

In the research proposal, you make a "contract" with your instructor about how you will develop your topic, and in Assignments 2 and 3 you must honor the contract. Therefore, a proposal can be written only after you have thought about and researched your topic carefully. Since Assignment 3 requires you to take a position on your topic, you must now decide on a position and find library sources that support it. Before writing the proposal, you should have a clear understanding of *facts,* the basis for Assignment 2, and *issues,* the basis for Assignment 3. This difference will be explained to you later in this chapter.

The following research proposal was written by Teck-Ann Tan. His Assignment 3 is included in Chapter 9.

PROPOSAL

Thesis Statement for Assignment 3: The high rate of homicides in the United States is probably due to the lack of strict handgun control.

In Assignment 2, I will provide statistics regarding the number of deaths related to handguns. For instance, in 1988, there were 9,000 handgun-related deaths in the United States. About 400 deaths occurred in Washington, D.C., alone. I will also provide statistics on the number of handguns in the country, and describe city, state, and federal regulations currently in force to control handguns.

In Assignment 3, I will support my thesis by comparing the statistics for handgun-related deaths in the United States with statistics for Canada and Great Britain, countries that have strict handgun-control laws. I will also discuss the National Rifle Association's (NRA) role in this context, and show how the extensive financial resources of the NRA have prevented handgun-control laws from being adopted by Congress and state legislatures. I will also show why some of the regulations in force are ineffective. I will conclude with an argument for strict handgun control at state and federal levels.

WORKING BIBLIOGRAPHY

Blose, James. "State Programs for Screening Handgun Buyers." *Annals of the American Academy of Social and Political Science*. Ed. Richard D. Lambert. New York: May, 1981.

Cook, Philip J. "The Effect of Gun Availability on Violent Crime Patterns." *Annals of the American Academy of Political and Social Science*. Ed. Richard D. Lambert. New York: May, 1981.

Fauntroy, Walter E. "Should Manufacture and Sale of Handguns for Private Use Be Prohibited in the United States?" *Congressional Digest* Dec. 1990: 304–08.

"Have Gun, Will Shoot." *The Economist* 23 Jan. 1988: 23.

Kleinman, Joel C. "International and Interstate Comparisons of Homicide Among Young Males." *Journal of the American Medical Association* 7 Nov. 1990: 3292–3295.

Mikva, Abner J. "Should Manufacture and Sale of Handguns for Private Use be Prohibited in the United States?" *Congressional Digest* Dec. 1990: 300–03.

Pierce, Glenn L. "The Bartetley-Fox Gun Law's Short-Term Impact on Crime in Boston." *Annals of the American Academy of Political and Social Science*. Ed. Richard D. Lambert. New York: May, 1981.

Robertson, Ian. *Sociology*. New York: Wort, 1988.

United States Dept. of Justice. *Sourcebook of Criminal Justice*. Washington: GPO, 1990.

Zimring, Franklin E. *Firearms and Violence in American Life*. Washington: Dale, 1969.

EXERCISE 8.1   WRITING A RESEARCH PROPOSAL

Write a proposal explaining how you plan to write on the topic you have chosen. Your proposal should include (a) a tentative thesis statement for Assignment 3, (b) an explanation of how you will support your thesis in Assignments 2 and 3, and (c) a working bibliography. For the working bibliography, present 10 sources that deal with your research paper topic. These sources should be books and periodical articles that you think could be used in your research paper. Remember to make a copy of the proposal for your files.

UNDERSTANDING FACTS AND ISSUES

In the sample research proposal just given, the thesis statement indicates what information will be contained in Assignments 2 and 3 and how this information will be organized. The thesis statement "The high rate of homicides in the United States is probably due to the lack of strict handgun control" means that the writer will have to include information on the number of homicides in the United States, compare this rate with homicides in other countries (to show that the U.S. rate is high), relate the homicides to handguns, and argue that handgun-control laws in the United States are not strict enough. As you can see, the writer will have to combine facts (comparable homicide rates, handgun-control laws) with issues (Are handgun-control laws in the United States not strict enough? Is the high rate of homicide in the United States due to lax laws?) in order to argue the thesis.

Assignment 3, Writing to Persuade, is where you use all the facts you have collected to argue your point of view. To prepare for this argument, you present some of the information you have collected through library research in Assignment 2, Writing to Inform. Since you already have a point of view, as stated in the thesis statement in the research proposal, the facts you collect should be relevant to your thesis and should enable you to support the thesis. However, some students confuse *facts* and *issues,* so the purpose of this section is to help you understand the difference between the two and show you how to use facts to argue in support of issues.

To show you the difference between facts and issues, we have taken thesis statements from three research proposals. You will read more about facts and issues in Chapter 9.

Research Proposal 1

Thesis Statement: Solar energy, which is safe and clean, may be the best substitute for coal.

Fact: Solar energy is safe and clean.

Issue: Solar energy may be the best substitute for coal.

As you can see, the thesis statement for Assignment 3 contains both facts and issues. The factual part of the thesis statement can be used for Assignment 2. For example,

Assignment 2 Thesis Statement (Fact): Solar energy is safe and clean.

Research Proposal 2

Thesis Statement: Europe, which is now united, may become the next superpower.

Fact: Europe is now united.

Issue: Europe may become the next superpower.

Assignment 2 Thesis Statement (Fact): Europe is now united.

Research Proposal 3

Thesis Statement: Millions of people go hungry every day probably because grains are fed to animals.

Fact: Millions of people go hungry every day.

Issue: This may be because grains are fed to animals.

Assignment 2 Thesis Statement (Fact): Millions of people go hungry every day.

ANALYZING THESIS STATEMENTS   **EXERCISE 8.2**

Read the following thesis statements for Assignment 3. Working with a partner or in a small group, decide if the thesis statements contain issues. If they don't, explain why. The thesis statements for Assignment 2 (facts) are in boldface type.

1. **To sell cigarettes to other countries** is to kill many innocent people and be irresponsible.

2. **Instead of research,** the Indian government should put more emphasis on public education and awareness to prevent the spread of AIDS.

3. **The enormous energy needs** make nuclear power essential to the world. But the world's political turmoil demands a careful control of nuclear power exploitation.

(continued)

(continued)

4. **Despite many social, economic, and political advances in Latin America,** I believe that the women of the region still face discrimination.

5. **AIDS in Africa and Asia is increasing.** It may be the fastest growing disease in the world.

6. **AIDS is no longer someone else's problem.** Facts about AIDS might save your life.

7. **The ethnic diversity of Malaysia** may be a positive factor in the country's development.

8. **After the disintegration of the Soviet Union, the United States is the only military superpower.** However, the economic and political situation may be more complex because of countries like Japan and Germany.

METHODS OF DEVELOPMENT

In Chapter 6, you learned to develop a topic by using description, narration, and examples. As you progress into academic writing, you will use other methods as well to develop a topic, such as definition and classification. In this chapter, you will learn how to use definition and classification in informative writing.

Definition

In attempting to describe or argue about a topic, writers often have to define unfamiliar terms, concepts, or objects to their readers. There are many kinds of definitions, but the most commonly used in writing are informal definitions, formal (sentence) definitions, and expanded definitions.

Informal Definitions

You could use **informal definitions** when a close synonym or examples exist for the word you want to define. The definition is enclosed within parentheses or commas. For example:

The effervescent (bubbling) mixture is highly toxic.

The Japanese Diet (or parliament) was officially opened on November 25, 1890.

Some industrialized countries, such as the United States, Canada, and Australia, have food surpluses.

Formal (Sentence) Definitions

Formal (sentence) definitions are the kind most often found in textbooks and dictionaries. Instead of the definition being placed within commas or parentheses, a sentence or clause is created solely for the purpose of defining a word. For example:

Asphalt is a mixture of hydrocarbons that is used for road building.

A third source of renewable energy is geothermal energy, which is heat trapped in rocks and fluids beneath the earth's surface.

Expanded Definitions

An **expanded definition** is a definition that may take several sentences to complete. You may want to use expanded definitions when informal or formal definitions are not sufficient to define a word or a concept. For example:

Solar energy is of two kinds: photovoltaic and solar thermal. Photovoltaic cells convert sunlight directly into electricity. Solar thermal energy is generated by solar collectors which concentrate sunlight and convert it to electricity.

Purdah comes from a root word meaning "veil" or "curtain." It refers to the custom of secluding women and enforcing certain high standards of female modesty. It is the usual explanation given for the absence of Muslim women in public places. Some say that this practice dates back to the time of the Prophet Muhammad. Others claim it did not take hold until the eighth century when a profligate ruling class began to hide their innumerable wives and concubines from public view. In any event, purdah has been a custom in the Muslim world for fourteen hundred years. (Amir K. Shafi)

WRITING DEFINITIONS   **EXERCISE 8.3**

Select three of the following topics. With a partner, write formal definitions for two of the topics and an extended definition for the third topic.

acid rain	hematite	neolithic
greenhouse effect	hemophilia	hydropower

Classification

One strategy for organizing information so that it is easy to understand is **classification**—dividing a large group of items into smaller groups of similar items.

Let's take cars as an example. The cars we see on campus can be classified according to the manufacturer (such as GM, Ford, Chrysler, Honda, etc.) or according to whether they were manufactured in the United States or abroad.

Classification can be a useful way to analyze information. It can also serve as an organizational strategy for papers that you may write both in school and on the job. An engineer, for example, might write a manual describing a machine. Classifying the machine according to its component parts, or according to its various systems, would be a useful way to organize the manual. If you look carefully at the way this book is organized, you will see how classification has been used.

How to Classify

To see how classification might work, let's discuss again how we might analyze the cars on campus. We could classify the cars according to the following principles:

foreign versus domestic

late model versus older cars (we would have to define what we mean by "late model")

luxury, medium-priced, and economy cars (again, we would have to define these terms, perhaps in terms of cost)

You can see that when we classify items, we often have to provide careful definitions or criteria for our categories. For the three possible bases for classification of cars just given, even the first, foreign versus domestic, is not as clear as it seems at first. How would we classify cars produced in the United States by foreign companies such as Honda and Toyota?

When you classify items into groups, you must clearly define the principles of classification. In addition, your classification must be consistent, exclusive, and complete.

Consistency: The groups must all be based on the same principle of division.

Exclusiveness: The groups must not overlap.

Completeness: All important examples must be included in the classification.

To help you plan the classification, you may find it helpful to draw a diagram such as the following:

Domestic Cars Classified According to Manufacturer

Ford	Chrysler	GM
Taurus	Dodge	Buick
Escort	Plymouth	Pontiac
etc.	etc.	etc.

CLASSIFYING TOPICS   EXERCISE 8.4

Pick at least two of the following topics, and working with a partner, classify each topic into two groups according to two or three principles of classification. Diagram your classifications, and be sure that they are consistent, exclusive, and complete.

teachers	movies	crimes
restaurants	team sports	climates

Purpose and Audience

When you analyze information through classification, you will often have choices about the principle of classification you use. To decide on the best principle, consider your reason for classifying the material and the people who will use this information. That is, consider the purpose of the writing and the needs and interests of your readers.

Let's assume that you are classifying the users of vehicles on campus. The information will be used by the campus administration for planning parking on campus. The purpose of your analysis would be to help ensure that parking is adequate for the various vehicle users. The most useful principle of classification in this example would be according to faculty/staff, students, disabled faculty/staff, disabled students, visitors, and university vehicles.

DECIDING ON PURPOSE AND AUDIENCE   EXERCISE 8.5

Look again at the classifications you diagramed for Exercise 8.4. Working with a partner, decide on a possible purpose and audience for each classification.

USING GRAPHICS

Many writers use tables and figures in their papers. Tables and figures are usually called **graphics**. A *graphic* is a visual form of presenting information, as opposed to words and numbers.

Graphics can be created easily with computer-aided design programs and inserted into your papers. However, use graphics only if you think they will help your readers understand your paper more easily.

What are the advantages of using graphics in your papers?

- Graphics provide a welcome break to the reader, weary after pages filled with words.
- Graphics emphasize important information. The appearance of a graphic in a paper signals to the reader that the writer wishes to emphasize a point.
- Graphics are often easier to understand than words.
- Graphics, such as tables, can summarize large amounts of information from pages of text and display them effectively.

Follow these guidelines when you use graphics in your papers:

- Place the graphic as close as possible to its first reference in your paper. For example, if you first referred to Table 1 on page 3, place Table 1 on page 3.
- Number the graphic (as Table 1 or Figure 1), and compose a title describing the contents of the graphic. Place the title *above* the table and *below* the figure.
- Place tables flush to the left margin or centered on the page; whichever way you choose, be consistent throughout the paper. Place figures centered on the page.
- In tables, name each column (the vertical lines) and row (the horizontal lines) carefully.
- Place the entire table on one page; don't continue the table from one page to another.
- Explain the contents of the graphic in your writing. But the graphic should also be self-sufficient; that is, the reader should be able to understand the graphic by itself.
- Identify the sources below the graphic, as in the list of Works Cited.
- Separate the graphic from the writing with enough white space so that the page does not look crowded.

ASSIGNMENT 2: WRITING TO INFORM

Your second writing assignment, a descriptive paper, will reflect the writing skills you have acquired thus far, with emphasis on definition and classification learned in this chapter.

You have already selected a research topic, expressed your knowledge and opinion on this topic in Assignment 1, and written a proposal on how you will develop the topic for Assignments 2 and 3.

For Assignment 2, assume that your classmates have assigned you to read a minimum of two sources (newspaper or periodical articles) on this topic and to report back to class all the important and relevant information contained in the sources.

Write a 500-word paper in which you combine the information you have gathered. This is strictly an informative paper; Assignment 3 will be argumentative. Your thesis statement should guide you in choosing relevant material from your sources.

You may use description and narration, examples, paraphrase, summary, quotations, definition, and classification in writing the paper; clarity, cohesiveness, and correct grammar and mechanics are also important.

Remember to title your paper, to cite your sources parenthetically, and to indicate the sources in a Works Cited section. The paper should be typed or computer-written and double-spaced. Your instructor will tell you when your first draft and final version are due. (Please submit the first draft with the final version.)

READINGS

To help you write Assignment 2, we have included five papers written by students. As you read these papers, note how the writers have used thesis statements to express their ideas, and methods of development, such as examples, description and narration, definition, and classification, to develop the ideas. Also note how sources have been used and acknowledged through the use of paraphrase, summary, and quotations. The study questions at the end of each paper will guide you in group discussions.

MEIJI, MOTHER OF MODERN JAPAN

Nita Bavikati

The sixties was a comfortable time for the United States. American companies prospered to no end, supplying "over three-quarters of the television sets, half the motor cars, and a quarter of the steel used around the world" ("High Technology" 3). However, something went terribly wrong in the next two decades. The American trade balance "went from a surplus of $5 billion in 1960 to a deficit of $150 billion in 1985" ("High Technology" 3). What went wrong? The answer lies with a group of small islands in the Pacific known as Japan. Today, Japan is considered an industrial giant, exceeded in industrial strength only by the United States and Russia.

Before the twentieth century, Japan was a little known country, possessing no significant social, political, or economic clout in world affairs.

The Japanese were not allowed to have any contact with foreigners, even through letters. Penalties were severe and applied to the whole family (Walworth 5). However, within a short period of time, Japan has grown to be a major world power and the isolation has ended. The beginning of this transition can be traced to the time Japan was ruled by Emperor Meiji. In fact, the Meiji period was responsible for Japan's initial modernization at social, political, and economic levels.

First, Japan's modernization at a social level began when the Meiji government decided to rectify, and later abolish, the feudal class system. For a start, the Meiji government made education universal. Before 1868, education was for the rich, only sons of the elite classes being allowed to seek a higher education (Sansom 476). During the Meiji period, "[e]ven sons from poorer homes were accepted [into universities] on the basis of their ability, without regard to social status or wealth" (Yoshida 26). In addition to universal education, the government also guaranteed freedom of choice in occupation and marriage to all members of society. Further, the Meiji government decided that it would draft anyone into military service regardless of class distinction. Earlier, only members of the warrior class were allowed to participate in the military (Yoshida 75).

In addition to these social changes, the Meiji period also brought about major political developments. The Japanese government was modernized in thought as well as structure. During the Meiji period, political issues became predominant in the social and intellectual lives of the people (Sansom 328). As a result, by the 1890s, the Japanese had already formed well-organized political parties (Akita 67). In addition to political thought, the political structure was also modernized. The days of central feudalism were replaced by a parliamentary system. The Diet, or parliament, was officially opened on November 25, 1890 (Akita 76). The Lower and Upper Houses of the Diet formed the legislative branch of the government. The executive branch consisted of the administrative, religious, financial, military, and diplomatic departments. Later, the Department of Internal Affairs was added (Akamatsu 239). The third branch of the government was the judiciary. This political structure in Meiji Japan is similar to many of today's governments, including that of Great Britain.

Finally, the Meiji government also brought about major economic development. Before the Meiji period, the Japanese economic system was very unreliable and inconsistent and under Meiji, the economy was reformed. The banking system was unified with the establishment of a central bank (Ohkawa and Rosovsky 11). Before the Meiji period, land had been taxed according to the needs of the local lord, the official who collected taxes in his province. This system of land tax was very inconsistent and there was no guarantee that farmers would be able to retain any increase in agricultural production. However, the Meiji government rectified this situation by imposing land taxes according to the value of the land (Ohkawa and Rosovsky 13–14).

In conclusion, Japan's initial modernization at social, economic, and political levels was due to the Meiji period. Imagine that the Meiji era never existed. Would Japan still have maintained its complete isolationist policy? Would Japan be a little known, underdeveloped Third World nation? Of course, this is just supposition, but it merits speculation.

WORKS CITED

Akamatsu, Paul. *Japan–History–Restoration, 1853–1870*. New York: Harper & Row, 1972.

Akita, George. *Foundations of Constitutional Government in Modern Japan, 1868–1900*. Cambridge: Harvard UP, 1967.

"High Technology: Clash of the Titans." *The Economist* 23 Aug. 1986: 3–5.

Ohkawa, Kazushi, and Henry Rosovsky. *Japanese Economic Growth: Trend Acceleration in the Twentieth Century*. London: Oxford UP, 1973.

Sansom, G. B. *The Western World and Japan*. London: Cresset, 1950.

Walworth, Arthur. *Black Ships Off Japan*. New York: Knopf, 1946.

Yoshida, Shigeru. *Japan's Decisive Century, 1867–1967*. New York: Praeger, 1967.

Study Questions for Nita Bavikati's Paper

1. What is the thesis statement of Bavikati's paper?

2. What are the topic sentences for paragraphs 3, 4, and 5?

3. Do paragraphs 3, 4, and 5 support the thesis?

4. What is the purpose of paragraph 1?

5. Has this writer provided enough facts to support her thesis?

6. An informative paper should contain only facts, not the author's opinion. Do you think this paper is limited to facts?

ETHNIC AND RELIGIOUS VIOLENCE IN NIGERIA

Michael K. Nsah

The birth of Nigeria on October 1, 1960, after a long stretch of British colonial rule, was like the break of a new dawn for the continent of Africa. It was viewed by the world as a step towards a progressive and formidable Black Africa (Northcott 1463). However, this hope was dashed to the wind by a tragic and ill-timed incident barely six years later, when Nigeria was thrown into a civil war that was precipitated by ethnic and religious violence that erupted in the north. What a trauma, borne out of intolerance between two of Nigeria's three main ethnic groups who some months back called each other fellow countrymen! These catastrophic circumstances left Nigeria in a position where it could not reach out to help other African countries in need. After all, can a man who does not know how to swim help another who is drowning?

Nigeria's ethnic problem dates back to the pre-independence era. Nigeria, as a nation, is a child of British colonialism, and did not exist as an entity before the amalgamation of the southern and northern provinces in 1914 by the British. Even its name was given by Lady Lugard, wife of the country's first governor-general. Population wise, Nigeria has approximately 120 million, occupying an area the size of Alabama, Florida, Georgia, and Tennessee combined. The northern region is larger than the eastern and western regions put together. The major ethnic groups are the Hausas and the Fulanis in the north, the Ibos in the east, and the Yorubas in the west. In fact, there are over 250 tribes in Nigeria, and each of these tribes represents an ethnic group with diverse interests. So the three major ethnic groups can only swallow the minority groups with the same comfort and success as a man swallowing a fish bone.

For millions of Nigerians, the celebration of her independence in 1960 and the declaration of Nigeria as a republic in 1963 were extraordinary experiences. However, the hope was short lived. Anarchy struck in January 1966 when a bloody coup d'etat claimed the lives of notable Nigerian leaders. Among the victims were "Federal Prime Minister Abubakar Tafawa Balewa, who came from the north, the Northern Premier Ahmadu Bello and the Western Premier Samuel Akintola." (Arthur 222). To add salt to the wounds of the agonizing northerners and westerners, an Ibo army officer, Major General Johnson Thomas Ironsi, took over the mantle of Nigeria's leadership. Obviously no one needed divine wisdom to know that the January 1966 coup was rooted in the insatiable ethnic interest of a few to the detriment of the Nigerian populace.

The northerners and the westerners were poised for revenge. By April of the same year, there were reports of widespread riots in the north. The young Ibo military officers in power did not know that the uprising was a smoldering inferno perpetrated against the Ibos. The riot left 30,000 Ibo men, women and children dead ("A New Country" 84). On July 29, the northern military officers staged their coup. This time the military head of state, Major General Ironsi, was killed and Lt. Col. Yakubu Gowon, a northerner, became the head of state. The table had now turned. The Ibos were on the receiving end of the agony. This forced the military governor of the eastern region, on the advice of the joint Ibo leaders' session, to decree that the eastern region had become an independent state effective May 27, 1967 (Arthur 223). The head of state, Yakubu Gowon, who by now was a general, immediately decided to divide the four regions into twelve states: six in the north, three in the east, two in the west, and one in the midwest. As the tension mounted, all the states in the east decided to secede and become the Republic of Biafra. All of this chaos led to "Black Africa's first modern war" ("Tragedy in the Villages" 37). It was a very traumatic experience for the Ibos in particular. Nigeria became the testing ground for some post–World War II weapons. Britain and Russia were on the Nigerian side, while France was on the Biafran side.

The magnitude of the sufferings heightened for the Ibos. It ranged from mass starvation to bombing attacks, and the death toll was in the neighborhood of 6,000 daily (Arthur 221). Naked children with swollen bellies were seen all over the refugee camps ("Tragedy in the Villages" 38). The inflation rate skyrocketed due mainly to economic instability. Basic daily meals were inaccessible, even though Nigeria is blessed with abundant natural and human resources ("A New Country" 82–84). Most of the people were totally broken emotionally. Some who could not bear the emotional pain and agony died as a result. What is more, I lost the dearest person in my life, my mother, who could not bear the separation from her family because she thought they had all been killed. In just twenty months of the Nigerian civil war, about 400,000 were killed (Arthur 224). This I believe did not include the soldiers who were also killed in no small numbers. The cost and adverse effect of the war is simply inestimable because of the human lives that were involved. As the popular African proverb goes, "When two elephants fight, it is the grass that gets trampled" (Arthur 224).

The period of the ethnically motivated war in Nigeria was a time when the religious fundamentalists and extremists were in limbo. But after the war was over in January 1970 and following a few years of reconstruction and rehabilitation, various religious sects started forming their coalitions. The north, predominantly Muslim, and the east, predominantly Christian, regrouped fast as if answering a trumpet call. Almost all matters in Nigeria were influenced by these two groups. For example, when the political parties were formed, they were based on ethnic, tribal, or religious bias. A further example is the composition of the very first political parties in the 60s. The Hausas and the Fulanis in the north, both of whom are Moslems, controlled the Northern People's Congress; the Ibos in the east, who are Christians, controlled the National Convention of Nigerian Citizens; while the Yorubas in the west, a mixture of Moslems and Christians, were in charge of the Action Group Party. This showed how deeply divided Nigeria had become and the effect that religion had on Nigeria's structural foundation.

In 1991, as in many times in the past, religious violence erupted in one of the major cities in the north and at least 120 people were slaughtered. Christians and Moslems took flight in the thousands for their dear lives. The confrontation that led to the incident was whether or not the Christians should be allowed to slaughter pigs, which the Moslems forbid, and dogs in a local abattoir ("Godly Slaughter" 47).

In effect, the spirit of ethnicity and religion have for long stood in the path of Nigeria's progress towards effective democracy. For instance, a free and fair election could be nullified simply because of a complaint from some ethnically or religious minded group. And that was exactly the case in the August 1993 presidential election. Fearing violence, the military head of state was forced to resign (Noble A3). It is disheartening that after all these traumatic experiences, the ghost of ethnic and religious intolerance in Nigeria has still not been buried.

WORKS CITED

"A New Country on the Rise Despite War." *U.S. News & World Report* 16 June 1969: 82–84.

Arthur, George. "Perspective on Nigeria." *America* 22 Feb. 1969: 221–25.

"Godly Slaughter." *The Economist* 4 May 1991: 47–48.

Noble, Kenneth B. "Nigerian Ruler Cedes Power to Civilian." *New York Times* 27 Aug. 1993: A3.

Northcott, C. "Africa's Future Leader." *Christian Century* Dec. 1960: 1463.

"Tragedy in the Villages." *Time* 7 Mar. 1969: 37–38.

Study Questions for Michael K. Nsah's Paper

1. What is the thesis of Nsah's paper?

2. What are the topic sentences for paragraphs 2, 3, and 4?

3. How does the author introduce the paper? How does he get the reader's attention at the beginning of the paper?

4. Is this paper just facts, or does the author add his opinion at some places within the paper?

5. What methods of development has Nsah used for his paper? Look for the use of examples, narration, description, personal experience, definition, and classification. (All of these methods of development may not be used in the paper.)

6. Do you think any parts of this paper need more development?

7. Find an example of a direct quotation in this paper.

8. Write an outline for this paper.

9. What do you like about Nsah's paper?

10. What suggestions do you have for improving this paper?

WOMEN OF THE VEIL: HAPPY OR OPPRESSED?

Amir K. Shafi

Purdah comes from a root word meaning "veil" or "curtain." It refers to the custom of secluding women and enforcing certain high standards of female modesty. It is the usual explanation given for the absence of Muslim women in public places. Some say that this practice dates back to the time of the Prophet Muhammad. Others claim it did not take hold until the eighth century when a profligate ruling class began to hide their innumerable wives and concubines from public view. In any event, purdah has been a custom in the Muslim world for fourteen hundred years (Warwick 462).

Purdah practices vary by country, region, class and even within the life span of an individual female. In Pakistan, for example, there are anomalies that characterize purdah. On farms, in the rural areas, where female labor is essential for survival, women work openly in the fields, yet in villages, the bazaar area remains out of bounds; women enter only if heavily veiled (Warwick 462).

As a general rule, the lower the economic class of the woman, the less likely she is to be veiled and vice versa. An explanation for this may be that people have less regard for the lower classes. On the other hand, the wife of a rich man, such as a rural landowner, has to veil herself because this is an indication that she comes from a rich family which does not require its women to work. In urban areas of Pakistan, the opposite appears to be true (Robinson 11).

Some women who live in cities like Karachi are liberal minded, as they are more in touch with the Western world, Western fashions, and Western thought. They move in society without a veil, sometimes even going to the extent of wearing clothes which show their form and figure. They believe in the Western notion that if a woman has a veil over her head, it is also covering her mind, thus not allowing her any intellectual growth. While they, along with the West, may believe that Islam has imposed these restrictions upon women to stop their intellectual growth, nothing can be further from the truth (Faquir 12).

The wives of the Prophet Muhammad were vibrant, outspoken women. His first, Hazrat Khadija, ran a prosperous trading business and at one point was Muhammad's employer. She was so independent that she herself asked for Muhammad's hand in marriage. Hazrat A'isha, the Prophet's favorite, was at various times a judge, a political activist, and a warrior. Her personality is so credible that most of the *hadiths* (sayings of the Prophet), on which the Muslim faith mainly rests, were narrated by her. Among Muhammad's eleven other wives and concubines were a leather worker, an *imam* (a religious leader) and an advocate of the downtrodden, revered in her days as the "Mother of the Poor" (Beyer 37).

But Islam also enshrined certain discriminatory practices. As decreed by the Koran, the value of a woman's testimony in court is worth half that of a man's, and men are entitled to four spouses, whereas women can have only one. Males are superior, some argue, because the Koran says they have "more strength" (Beyer 37).

Because of the Western expansionism in the 18th and 19th centuries, the Muslims feared the erosion of their culture. Because of this fear, the *Wahhabis* (a subgroup of Muslims) and others chose to assert values that set them apart, including the negative aspects of Islam's treatment of women. Modern Islamic fundamentalism is essentially a revival of their earlier reaction against the West (Beyer 37).

Despite such stifling interpretations of Islam, many women have found their liberation in their faith. The veil may be a symbol of oppression to the Western eye, but, to many who wear it, it is freedom—not just from the tyranny of Western culture but also from unwanted sexual advances.

WORKS CITED

Beyer, Lisa. "Life Behind the Veil." *Time* Fall 1990: 37.

Faquir, Fadia. "Unveiling Paradise." *New Statesman & Society* 18 Feb. 1992: 12–13.

Robinson, Melissa. "Unveiled." *The New Republic* 9 March 1992: 11.

Warwick, Ellen D. "The Veil Is Hard to Lift: Women's Place in Pakistan." *Commonweal* 9 Aug. 1991: 462.

Study Questions for Amir K. Shafi's Paper

1. What is the thesis of Shafi's paper?

2. What methods does Shafi use to develop his thesis? Look for the use of examples, narration, description, personal experience, definition, and classification. (All of these methods of development may not be used in the paper.)

3. Give examples of informal, formal, and expanded definitions from Shafi's paper.

4. Did you enjoy reading Shafi's paper? Why or why not?

5. Did the paper leave you with any unanswered questions?

6. How could Shafi have improved his paper?

AIDS IN AFRICA AND ASIA

Faisal Hussain

According to the World Health Organization (WHO), nearly 70 percent of the people infected with AIDS live in Africa (see Figure 1). Countries with a high rate of infection are Uganda, Burundi, Malawi, Rwanda, Tanzania, and Zambia (Weeks 208). WHO also reported that in 1992, Asia had 1 million individuals, mostly in India and Thailand, whose blood had tested positive for the AIDS virus (Steele 11). The fatal disease has spread over these continents quickly in the past ten years and the potential impact over the next decade could be devastating.

AIDS is caused by two types of virus known as HIV-1 (Human Immunodeficiency Virus Type 1) and HIV-2 (Human Immunodeficiency Virus Type 2). HIV-2 is more dangerous than HIV-1 and was first detected in West African prostitutes in 1985 (Weeks 209).

Uganda is the African country that is hardest hit by AIDS. A study of pregnant women conducted in Kampala, the capital city, showed that the infection rate had increased from 11 percent in 1985 to more than 25 percent in 1992. The women studied were a low-risk group (excluding prostitutes). Women in high-risk groups (prostitutes) had a 75 percent infection rate. The wave of infection is now spreading toward rural areas of Uganda (Weeks 208–13).

Asia, which has 60 percent of the world's population, has also seen the rapid spread of AIDS. In Bombay, a large city in India, it is estimated that 30,000 infected prostitutes serve 150,000 clients daily, exposing them to the risk of infection. In the words of one Indian scientist, "We are sitting on the top of a volcano" (qtd. in Goldsmith 1048). Prostitution, homosexuality, and extensive drug use, which are the usual ways in which AIDS is spread, are becoming a part of the Indian way of life (Steele 11).

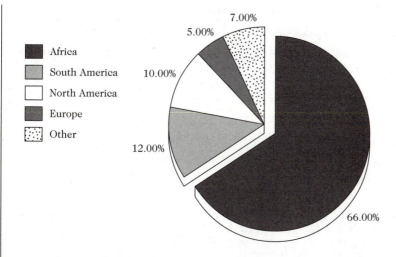

Africa
South America
North America
Europe
Other

7.00%
5.00%
10.00%
12.00%
66.00%

FIGURE 1 *Global distribution of HIV-infected adults, 1992 (Source: Weeks, Dennis. "The AIDS Pandemic in Africa."* Current History May *1992: 208–13.*

AIDS first appeared in Thailand among intravenous drug users a few years ago. By 1992, roughly 200,000 people in Thailand were believed to have been infected with AIDS (Goldsmith 1048). Burmese prostitutes who work in Thailand are the main carriers of AIDS to Burma. Since Burma's health facilities are poor and prostitution and drug use is prevalent, Burma could be the most vulnerable among Asian countries to AIDS (Lintner 31).

The problem is not so acute in Singapore, since it has few drug users. However, five million visitors pour into Singapore each year, and it is likely that these visitors may be infected by prostitutes (Goldsmith 1048). In Japan, 473 people were diagnosed with AIDS and 2,077 people had tested positive for the AIDS virus by 1992. However, experts believe that the actual number may be ten times larger (Mizuno 77).

The WHO and other organizations are fighting continuously against AIDS in Africa and Asia. However, considering the rate at which AIDS is spreading, the battle may already be lost.

WORKS CITED

Goldsmith, Marsha. "Rapid Spread of Pandemic in Asia Dismays Experts." *Journal of the American Medical Association* 28 Aug. 1991: 1048.

Lintner, Bertil. "Immigrant Viruses." *Far Eastern Economic Review* 20 Feb. 1992: 31.

Mizuno, Hajime. *What Is Scary About AIDS*. Tokyo: Chuokoron-sha, 1992.

Steele, Ian. "Danger in Asia." *World Press Review* Jan. 1992: 11.

Weeks, Dennis. "The AIDS Pandemic in Africa." *Current History* May 1992: 208–13.

Study Questions for Faisal Hussain's Paper

1. What is the thesis of Hussain's paper?

2. What methods does Hussain use to develop his thesis? Look for examples, narration, description, personal experience, definition, classification, and graphics. (All of these methods of development may not be used.)

3. Give examples of definitions from Hussain's paper.

4. Did you enjoy reading this paper? Why or why not?

5. Did the paper leave you with any unanswered questions?

6. How could Hussain have improved his paper?

WOMEN'S PLACE IN ISLAM

Syed Arafat Kabir

Is there any accepted human rights code in this world? The answer is yes. It constitutes freedom of speech and freedom of choice regardless of race and gender. However, in the Muslim world, some women are not being given their fair share of rights. The situation can best be described in the words of an Iranian lecturer who says, "It is easy to live as a woman in Iran as long as you first accept that you are worth half a man" ("Cover Up" 30). The root of this deprivation can be traced back to the legal structure of the Muslim world and its traditional values and beliefs.

The legal system of the Muslim world is based on the Sharia law (Islamic Law), which is comprised of the holy Koran, Sunna (the model behavior of the prophet), analogic reasoning (qiyas) and the consensus of the community (ijma) (*Law and Islam* 2). Despite the fact that the Koranic teachings and the Sharia laws are more inclined to improve women's rights than to exploit them (Mortley 108), the condition of the Muslim women has deteriorated because "self-appointed clerics and self-rejected regimes" abuse Islam continuously (Faquir 13). For instance, Sudan's pro-Islamic regime restrained a woman from leaving the country without being accompanied by her husband or brother or father. In 1985, the Egyptian Supreme Court struck down a law that gave a woman the right to divorce her husband should he take a second wife. The 1984 family code in Algeria gave a husband the right to divorce his wife for almost any cause and eject her from the residence (Beyer 37). Similar marriage contracts used in Iran lay down 16 circumstances for a woman to fulfill in order to get a divorce, whereas men can get a divorce without a reason ("Cover Up" 30).

In addition to the faulty legal structure, the traditional values and beliefs are also adverse to a woman's desire for freedom. In Iran, leaflets forbid women from showing more than their hands and faces ("Cover Up" 30). Women are arrested from streets for wearing cosmetics (Bordewich 85). Even in Britain's more liberal society, some Muslim women are being forced into arranged marriages and denied higher education (Bard 19). Many Imams (Muslim clergymen) think of women as objects of desire "lacking in rationality" (Faquir 12).

It is interesting that when women are striving to gain their rights, the reversals often come from fellow women. The Egyptian newspaper *Al-Muslimun* recently published an article written by Dr. Aisha Abdulrahman. Dr. Abdulrahman, a professor of religious sciences in Egypt, is quoted as saying that "women are lacking in mind and I am lacking although I have reached the highest academic rank" (Faquir 12).

Such compliance to male dominance creates unfortunate situations when progressive women seek to improve their lot. For instance, in Peshawar, Pakistan, more than a dozen Afghan women have been abducted by fundamentalist groups for the crime of working with foreign aid organizations; and a nurse in Mascara, Algeria, was burned to death by her brother for treating male patients (Beyer 37). Traditional values appear to severely restrict a woman's outward activities in some Muslim countries.

Naturally, the question arises whether such constraints are allowed by Islam. A careful study of the life styles of the prophet Muhammad (founder of Islam) and his spouses will reveal that the prophet advocated emancipation of women. He stopped female infanticide, made education of women a sacred duty, and ensured the right of a woman to "own and inherit property" (Beyer 37). The spouses of the prophet were outstanding women. His first, Khadija, was a successful merchant; and his favorite, Aisha, had assumed the positions of a judge, a political activist, and even a warrior at various times (Beyer 37). Pointing to his wife Aisha, the prophet himself told his followers to take "half their religion" from "that redhead" (Fernea 16). But nevertheless, women still continue to suffer in the Muslim world. Fadia Faquir, an exiled Muslim female writer, points out that "[b]etween us and Allah stand the self-appointed clerics whose 'holier than thou' techniques politicize Islam beyond recognition" (12).

The increasing fundamentalism in many Muslim countries is placing even more constraints on women. Apparently, this trend seems to be a revival of the reaction against Western expansionism in the 18th and 19th centuries. At that time, fearing the erosion of their culture, many Islamic sects adopted severe and specific rules that would set them apart (Beyer 37).

In the 1930s Picasso painted an Algerian woman "with the hall open and sunlight streaming in" (Fernea 7). What Picasso wanted to show on canvas was that Muslim women of Algeria were experiencing a life of prosperity and well-being. The picture is, however, different now although the world has advanced in every sphere. That may be why the Algerian writer Assia Djebar hopes that the view of Picasso will be the future of Muslim women (Fernea 12), the sunlight being education, freedom of speech, and choice; and the open door being the changed social order and a more realistic legal structure. In conclusion, one can only wish that Djebar's hope will be fulfilled in the future.

WORKS CITED

Bard, Julia. "The Priests Have It." *New Statesman & Society* 1 May 1992: 19.

Beyer, Lisa. "Life Behind the Veil." *Time* Fall 1990: 37.

Bordewich, Fergus M. "Inside Iran: Decade of Destruction." *Reader's Digest* Oct. 1992: 85.

"Cover Up, Quick: Iranian Women." *The Economist* 22 Aug. 1992: 30.

Faquir, Fadia. "Unveiling Paradise." *New Statesman & Society* 18 Feb. 1992: 12–13.

Fernea, Elizabeth W. *Women and the Family in the Middle East: New Voices of Change.* Austin: U of Texas P, 1985.

Law and Islam in the Middle East: New York: Bergin & Garvey, 1990.

Mortley, Raoul. *Womanhood: The Feminine in Ancient Hellenism, Gnosticism, Christianity, and Islam.* Sydney: Delacroix, 1981.

Nikki, Keddi, and Louis Beck. *Women in the Muslim World.* Massachusetts: Harvard UP, 1978.

Study Questions for Syed Arafat Kabir's Paper

1. Did you enjoy reading Kabir's paper? Why or why not?

2. Does Kabir restrict his paper to facts, or does he also include his opinions?

3. In your opinion, what are the strengths of Kabir's paper?

4. If you were peer-reviewing Kabir's paper, what suggestions would you make for improving his paper?

PLANNING/SELF-EVALUATION OF DRAFT

As in Chapter 6, we have included a Planning/Self-Evaluation of Draft form in order to help you with your paper. As you complete this form, you will think carefully about your paper. Your responses on the form will show you how your paper is going to be organized. The form can also be used to self-evaluate your draft before your classmates peer-review it. Items 7 to 11 are mainly for your self-evaluation.

PLANNING/SELF-EVALUATION OF DRAFT

1. Tentative title:

2. My purpose in this paper is to describe . . .

3. My thesis statement is:

4. My topic sentences are:

    1.

    2.

    3.

    4.

5. I have arranged the topic sentences in this order because:

6. The examples to support my topic sentences are:

    Topic sentence 1:

    Topic sentence 2:

    Topic sentence 3:

    Topic sentence 4:

7. I need to define the following terms:

8. I need to develop the following points/paragraphs:

9. I need to omit the section on _____ because . . .

10. My opening is effective because . . .

11. My closing is effective because . . .

PEER REVIEW

In Chapter 6, you peer-reviewed papers your classmates wrote. In reading those papers and giving advice on revision, you may have learned ways of improving your own paper for Assignment 1. In addition, the reviews you received on your paper should have helped you to make it better.

We also have provided a peer-review sheet for Assignment 2. Follow the instructions carefully. As in Assignment 1, write your comments and suggestions after reading your classmate's paper two or three times. Always offer specific comments and suggestions. You may write comments directly on the writer's paper.

When you have completed the peer-review sheet, go to the student whose paper you reviewed and further explain your comments and suggestions to him or her. Use the peer-review sheet to guide you in this discussion. Ask the writer questions; questions motivate writers to think critically.

ASSIGNMENT 2—PEER REVIEW

Author:

Reviewed by:

First, read the paper straight through to get a quick, general impression. On the second or third reading, respond to the paper according to the guidelines given below. Please offer specific comments. After writing your responses, discuss the paper with the writer. Thank you.

1. Did you enjoy the paper? (Yes or no). Why, or why not? Please be specific.

2. Is the title suitable for a 500-word paper? (Yes or no). If the title is too broad, how can it be narrowed?

3. Is the introduction effective? (Yes or no). Why or why not?

4. Is the thesis statement clear? (Yes or no). If not, how can it be clarified?

5. Are the topic sentences clear? (Yes or no).

6. Do the sentences in each paragraph relate to the topic sentence? (Yes or no).

7. Does the author use enough examples to develop his/her ideas? (Yes or no).

8. Is there any place in the paper where you were confused? (Yes or no). If yes, where and why?

9. Do any terms need to be defined? (Yes or no).

10. Is the ending effective? (Yes or no). If not, why?

11. Is the documentation of sources correct? (Yes or no).

12. How can this paper be improved?

REVISION

The following paper, "White Collar Crime" by Khurrum Qazi, will show you how a student revised the first draft of his paper. His revisions were based on the comments and suggestions he received from a classmate, his instructor, and tutors in the writing lab. The first draft, a peer review, and the final version of Qazi's paper are included.

WHITE COLLAR CRIME

Khurrum Qazi

Computers have led to white collar crime due to large use of and availability of them in the work place. The computer has spread to various types of organizations all over the world. The new computer networks in these institutions are making jobs more challenging than ever before.

Data processing was the extent of the mainframe computer in the recent past. Computers used to be more safe than they are now because they were sealed off in special rooms and the only one who operated them were the data processing managers. The computers were very safe and well protected. The room they were stored in was kept at a regular temperature and absolutely free from dust and other harmful substances. Now computers have become decentralized from the large special rooms of the past. There are now terminals in offices, on secretaries desks, and various other sites.

The most likely and most common threat to computer data is power failure. If you have a computer that is responsible for important devices such as fire alarms or machine tools you cannot afford to have power failure. The only way to secure your system from this type of security threat is to purchase battery back-up power, usually a weeks worth, to be safe. Power failure can be caused by many factors the most common is a storm. Other causes of power failure are surges and the power company working in the area. The second most common security threat is failure to backup or copy important data. This should not be a problem because the backup procedure does not take much time at all and is almost effortless. Reasons to backup is to save time and trouble in the long run when disaster happens.

Authority to access a computer is a rising problem because of the decentralization of computers. The problem is people being able to access the information or data that is supposed to be secure. These unauthorized accesses are protected by a password system or data encryption. A password system keeps out unauthorized people by requiring a code before being able to access the computer. This method has its flaws because people can figure out the password or it may just fall into the wrong hands. Data encryption is an electronic lock that uses algorithms to scramble the data. The ultimate security system, hopefully in the near future, will be a combination of voice identification and recognition technology. This would enable the user to access the computer voice rather than the keyboard and would enable the computer to keep a check on the identity of the user.

The problem lies with the decentralization of computers and the increasing knowledge of the common people about computer technology. There are many people working on this dilemma, but when they have a solution there is always someone smarter to find ways round the new security.

Here is the peer review Khurrum Qazi received from Inmaculada Diaz.

ASSIGNMENT 2—PEER REVIEW

Author: *Khurrum Qazi*

Reviewed by: *Inmaculada Diaz*

1. Did you enjoy the paper? (Yes or no). Why, or why not? Please be specific.

   I enjoyed some parts of the paper. But it was confusing.

2. Is the title suitable for a 500-word paper? (Yes or no). If the title is too broad, how can it be narrowed?

   The title is too broad. The title is "White Collar Crime," but the paper is about white collar crime committed with computers. I don't think all white collar crimes are committed with computers. Maybe you should title the paper "Computers and White Collar Crime."

3. Is the introduction effective? (Yes or no). Why, or why not?

   No. Third sentence in the first paragraph has nothing to do with the first sentence.

4. Is the thesis statement clear? (Yes or no). If not, how can it be clarified?

   I think the thesis statement is the first sentence in the opening paragraph. Yes, it is clear.

5. Are the topic sentences clear? (Yes or no).

   I could not find all the topic sentences. When reading the second paragraph, I thought you had misunderstood the term "white collar crime." The sentence "The room they were stored in was kept at a regular temperature" is not related to white collar crime.

6. Do the sentences in each paragraph relate to the topic sentence? (Yes or no).

   See comment in number 5.

7. Does the author use enough examples to develop his/her ideas?

   The examples are too general. Specific examples using facts and statistics would be better.

8. Is there any place in the paper where you were confused? (Yes or no). If yes, where and why?

   Yes, paragraphs 2 and 3 were confusing because they did not relate to the thesis.

9. Do any terms need to be defined? (Yes or no).

   A definition of "white collar crime" is needed.

10. Is the ending effective? (Yes or no). If not, why?

    I was confused by the time I came to the end.

11. Is the documentation of sources correct? (Yes or no).

    No.

12. How can this paper be improved?

    Get a clear idea of what white collar crime is. You should revise paragraph 2 and maybe delete paragraph 3 to make the paper clear. Write good topic sentences for each paragraph. Use more facts and statistics to support your examples.

The final version of Khurrum Qazi's paper is given below. Compare this version with the first draft you read earlier. What changes have been made? Why do you think Qazi made those changes? Does the paper need more revision?

title

STEALING WITH COMPUTERS

Khurrum Qazi

thesis

Embezzlement and fraud do not receive as much publicity as murders and bank robberies, but billions of dollars are stolen in these white collar crimes, which occur mostly in banks. In recent years, these crimes have increased due to a number of reasons.

topic sentence

background information

statistics

In 1965, four cases of embezzlement with computers were reported and ten years later, only 26 cases were reported (Ball 51). Although thousands of such crimes are committed every year now, authorities say that only about 10 percent of the cases are reported (Ball 95). It is estimated that every year, 200,000 such crimes take place in the U.S. costing about $5 billion. This figure is 20 times the loss of 20 years ago (Ball 101–2).

topic sentence

The typical embezzler is no different from the ordinary bank employee. The person is usually a middle-class citizen who has no previous criminal record (Johnson 280). It is estimated that 47 percent of computer crimes are committed by dishonest employees. The other crimes are due to accidents or ignorance of procedures (Staller 13). Donn B. Parker, an authority on computer crimes, says that a trustworthy employee who accidentally discovers a flaw in the bank's system can easily turn into a computer embezzler (Ball 47).

topic sentence

example

One reason for the increase in computer embezzlement is that the crime often goes unreported. Many banks remain silent, fearing that the bad publicity could affect their position in the stock market (Whiteside 35). Another worry is that depositors will lose confidence when they learn how often banks lose money in this manner (Bock 45). One extreme example of a case involving fear of publicity occurred at First Indiana National Bank. When an employee, who was a computer programmer, was caught stealing millions of dollars, the bank gave the man a letter of recommendation to help him find a new job. At the new job, he was caught embezzling $200 a week for three-and-a-half years. Once again, the man was not prosecuted (Whiteside 34).

topic sentence

examples

Another reason for the increase in embezzlement is that the punishment is not strong enough. For example, a head teller at the Union Dime Savings Bank branch in New York City, who stole $1.5 million, was sentenced to only two years in prison and served only 20 months. An employee at another bank who stole more than $1 million from customers' accounts was sentenced to 60 days in jail. He served 40 days and was released (Ball 60).

topic sentence

Perhaps the main reason for the increase in computer crimes is that authority to access a computer is fairly easy (Staller 13). People can access the information or data that is supposed to be secure. These accesses are protected by a password system or data encryption, which keeps out unauthorized users by requiring users to enter a code before being able to access the computer. The password system has its flaws because people can figure out the password or it may just fall into the wrong hands. Data encryption is an electronic lock that uses algorithms to scramble the data, and it is more secure (Johnson 53). The ultimate security system, hopefully in the near future, will be a combination of voice identification and recognition technology. This would enable the user to access the computer through voice rather than the keyboard and would enable the computer to keep a better check on the identity of the user (Johnson 192).

WORKS CITED

Ball, E. G. *Computer Auditing and Control.* New York: Petrocelli Charter, 1989. *book*

Bock, Gordon. "The Chairman and His Board; Embezzlers Nearly Get Away *article*
     with $69 Million from First Chicago." *Time* 30 May 1988: 45.

Johnson, E. H. *Handbook on Crime and Delinquency.* New York: Greenwood,
     1989.

Staller, Jay. "Computer Cops and Robbers." *Across the Board* June 1989: 13.

Whiteside, Thomas. "Annals of Crime: Dead Soul in Computer." *The New
     Yorker* 29 Aug. 1989: 34–37.

CHAPTER 9

Writing to Persuade

This chapter continues the research process you began in Chapter 8. You will learn to explore more sources in order to support the position you will argue on your research topic in Assignment 3.

This chapter also includes explanations of the purpose and audience for persuasive writing, methods of development for persuasive writing, and the format for a formal research paper. The chapter concludes with Assignment 3, related readings, and self-evaluation and a peer-review sheet.

A frequent assignment in academic writing is the research paper, which is usually based on library research and written according to a clearly defined format. Assignment 3 will be written according to this format, which will be explained later in the section "Research Paper Format."

The readings in this chapter will show you how some students have responded to this assignment. In "Gun Control: A Fundamental Step to Reduce the Rate of Gun-Related Deaths and Crime," Teck-Ann Tan argues that strict gun-control laws may reduce the crime and death rates in this country. In "African Famines: Can the Victims Be Saved?" Nelvy Espinoza argues that, although a solution to African famines appears to be impossible anytime soon, the number of victims may be reduced by the development of agriculture in Africa, a fairer treatment of African products in the world market, and a better utilization of African resources.

PURPOSE AND AUDIENCE

Why should you write to persuade? Usually, it is to inform your readers about a topic, express your opinions on the topic, and persuade the readers to accept your position or at least take it seriously. The examples given below show how two writers wrote persuasive papers by using various methods of development. The examples also show how these writers adjusted their writing in order to clarify the topics for their readers.

In a letter written to the chair of the biology department at her university, a student asks that she be allowed to substitute a microbiology course she took at another university for one required by the department. In the letter, the student compares the course description of the course she has already taken with the description of the course offered by the university where she is currently enrolled. She points out that the classroom and lab hours of both courses are equivalent, as are the topics covered.

In a research paper written for her freshman English class, a student argues for strict laws to control the ownership of handguns in the United States. She begins by citing statistics which show that since 1900, more Americans have been killed by privately owned handguns than have died in all the wars in United States history. At the beginning, she defines the term *handgun*. Knowing that her readers are ESL students, she explains the term *NRA* (for the National Rifle Association), which is mentioned often in her paper. She also explains the Second Amendment, which is often quoted by opponents of gun control. She uses a number of arguments, and also acknowledges and refutes counterarguments to strengthen her position. She includes numerous quotations, facts, and statistics in the paper. Stating that the United States is fast becoming the murder capital of the civilized world, she concludes her paper by arguing that strict handgun control would be a step in the right direction to stop the trend.

METHODS OF DEVELOPMENT

In Chapters 6 and 8, you learned to develop a topic by using description, narration, examples, definition, and classification. In this chapter, you will study how to use comparison and contrast and argumentation in persuasive writing.

Comparison and Contrast

In persuasive writing, comparison and contrast is often used to develop a topic. Soon after arriving in the United States, you may have written papers comparing your culture with American culture or the system of education in your country with that of the United States. When you compare two cultures or two educational systems, you soon see their differences too. **Comparison** shows the similarity between two things; **contrast** shows the difference.

We can see how writers have used comparison and contrast to develop their topics in the readings included in this chapter. Teck-Ann Tan begins his paper on gun control by comparing the United States handgun homicide rate to that of other industrialized countries such as England, Japan, Sweden, and Canada. By stating that the United States homicide rate is 77 times that of the other countries, Tan quickly points out the contrast in the statistic and goes on to argue in favor of gun control. Later in his paper, Tan compares the handgun homicide rate of Canada with that of the United States to emphasize his point of view.

In her paper on African famines, Nelvy Espinoza uses facts for comparison and contrast. She states that, although the number of Africans who died of famine in 1991 was ten times the number of Kurds displaced by the Gulf War, the media gave more publicity to the Kurdish situation than to the famine in Africa. Later in the paper, Espinoza compares the food situation in Africa with that in the United States. She states that while millions of Africans starve, Americans use grain to feed livestock and pumpkins to make funny faces (during Halloween).

As you can see, using facts and statistics for comparison and contrast will help you to strengthen your arguments, which is the next method of development to be discussed.

Argumentation

In academic writing, an **argument** should be based on an issue, and it should also be carefully reasoned and well supported. It should also take into account other points of view, or *counterarguments,* which we discuss later in this chapter.

In Chapter 8, we saw the difference between facts and issues. **Facts** are not arguable because they can be verified objectively. For instance, "Europe was recently united" is a fact because we know that a number of European nations signed an agreement in 1992 to form an economic union. We have read this in newspapers and magazines and have seen it reported or being discussed on television. The statement "Millions of people go hungry every day" is also a fact because it is reported in reliable books, magazines, and newspapers and because statistics on the number of hungry people are available.

Nonacademic arguments are often based on personal feelings. This is especially true when speakers or writers have strong feelings on a particular subject. Although personal feelings can be explained to others, such feelings are purely subjective and are therefore not arguable in an academic paper.

For instance, you may have a strong dislike for certain required courses in your academic program. You may be able to explain your feelings to others, but they may not agree with you because your feelings may be entirely subjective. However, you may be able to turn your feelings into a sound argument by stating that "some required courses may be unnecessary." Now you are in a position to argue why courses in foreign languages may not be necessary for a nursing major or why electrical engineers may have no use for courses in the humanities.

Issues, in contrast to facts, are arguable. For instance, in the statement "Solar energy, which is safe and clean, *may be the best substitute for coal,"* the italicized phrase neither is a fact nor is based on personal feelings. It is therefore an issue that can be argued. However, not everyone will agree that solar energy is the best substitute for coal, since alternative sources of energy such as wind and biomass are also available. Therefore, the issue is not stated emphatically. The qualifier *may* opens the issue to debate. Readers will be more accepting of the position taken on an issue if it is qualified with the use of such terms as *may, seems, apparently,* and *probably*.

THESIS STATEMENTS WITH QUALIFIERS   **EXERCISE 9.1**

Working with a partner or in a small group, read the thesis statements in Exercise 8.2. Are the statements properly qualified? If not, rewrite the statements with suitable qualifiers.

Supporting Issues with Quotations, Facts, and Statistics

In academic writing, issues are always supported by quoting authorities and citing facts and statistics.

Since freshman writers are not experts on the issues they argue, they need to *quote authorities* in order to strengthen their arguments. For example, in her research paper on African famines, Nelvy Espinoza quotes an authority in the following manner.

> However, Lathardus Goggins, Professor of African Studies at the University of Akron, argues that

>> despite this gloomy picture, Africa can draw encouragement from Third World models, including its own. India and China, for example, in the face of grievous economic obstacles, succeeded in growing enough food to supply populations greater than that of all Africa. Botswana launched a famine relief program that worked. Zimbabwe, aided by rain and strong leadership, reversed its food production decline. ("Africa: Environmental" 259)

Note how Espinoza gives the full name of the authority (Lathardus Goggins) and his affiliation (Professor of African Studies at the University of Akron) in the introduction to the quotation. She thus establishes the credentials of the authority she is quoting in support of her argument.

As stated earlier, facts can be verified objectively and are therefore not arguable. But, like quotations from authorities, facts can be used to support an argument. For instance, in the following paragraph, the writer uses facts to support his argument that Germany cannot become the next superpower.

> Germany, the largest economic power in the EEC, was reunited only in 1990. Before the reunification, East Germany's economy was in ruins, and there were wide gaps in the standard of living, technology, and consumer prices between the two Germanys. As a result of having to absorb its weak half, Germany is now facing a rise in inflation and unemployment.

In the following paragraph, the writer uses facts to support her statement that the Meiji period brought about major political developments in Japan.

> During the Meiji period, political issues became predominant in the social and intellectual lives of the people (Sansom 328). As a result, by the 1890s, the Japanese had already formed well-organized political parties (Akita 67). In addition to political thought, political structure was also modernized. The days of central feudalism were replaced by a parliamentary system. The Diet, or parliament, was officially opened on November 25, 1890 (Akita 76).

In addition to quoting authorities and citing facts, writers often cite **statistics** to support their arguments. In the following paragraph, the writer cites statistics to support his argument for strict handgun-control laws.

> The second reason for strict gun-control laws is the high rate of handgun homicide. In 1988, of the 18,269 homicides in the United States, 10,296, or 61 percent, were committed with guns. In Canada, a country with strict gun-control laws, only 27 percent of the murders were gun related. (Kleinman 3293)

When a large number of statistics have to be presented, a table is a more effective way of presenting the information. In her research paper on African famines, Espinoza presents statistics relevant to the paper in a table.

TABLE 1: *Impact of World Market Prices on African Agricultural Products*

Leading Products	1989 Price	Export Rate	1990 Price	Export Rate
Sugarcane	.475	65.7%	.455	59.8%
Bananas	.330	64.0%	.383	67.6%
Oranges	.737	70.4%	.776	72.3%
Peanuts	.215	16.5%	.197	10.4%
Cotton	.835	73.8%	.818	65.2%

Source: *The Europe World Year Book,* 1991, Vol. II.

Using Counterarguments

In the statement "Solar energy, which is safe and clean, may be the best substitute for coal," the writer acknowledges that not everyone will agree that solar energy is the best substitute for coal, since alternative sources of energy such as wind and biomass are also available. This acknowledgment is made by using the qualifier *may*. To show their readers that they are thoroughly informed about their topic, including both sides of the issue, persuasive writers also refer to points of view that are in opposition to their own position. Such opposing views to a writer's arguments are called **counterarguments.**

In Chapter 8, we saw how the thesis statements for three research proposals could be split into facts and issues. The issues are arguable. In other words, a person who disagrees with this position could offer counterarguments. Study the following examples for positions taken on arguable issues, with possible counterarguments that could arise.

Example 1—Thesis Statement (issue):

Solar energy, which is safe and clean, may be the best substitute for coal.

Two counterarguments that arise from such an issue could be stated as follows:

1. Solar energy is not available around the year.
2. To meet the energy needs of the United States, collector plates the size of Delaware will be necessary.

Example 2—Thesis Statement (issue):
Europe, which is now united, may become the next superpower.

At least two counterarguments that arise from such an issue could be:

1. East Asian countries will be more powerful than Europe.
2. Europe will never be one nation. Therefore, it cannot be a superpower.

Example 3—Thesis Statement (issue):
Millions of people go hungry every day probably because grains are fed to animals.

Two counterarguments that arise from such an issue could be stated as follows:

1. People go hungry because the world is overpopulated.
2. Even when food is available, poor storage and distribution cause much waste. As a result, people starve.

Unless writers anticipate counterarguments, their arguments will be one-sided and will not be taken seriously by readers. **Acknowledging** and, if possible, **refuting** counterarguments is essential in academic writing.

In the following example, Teck-Ann Tan, who argues for strict gun control in his research paper, first acknowledges a counterargument and then refutes it.

When discussing gun control, those who oppose such actions will cite a number of reasons for opposing gun control. First, they say that even without a gun, a murder can still be committed. However, this may not be the case. According to Glen L. Pierce, Director of the Center for Applied Research at Northeastern University, the Bartetley-Fox gun law "reduced gun homicide with no increase in non-gun homicide" in Boston (120). According to the Federal Bureau of Investigation (FBI), almost two-thirds of all killings in 1973 resulted from arguments between friends or among family members. Most of these killings might have ended with nothing more than a fistfight if there had been no gun in the house. Furthermore, one out of five gun attacks ends in death, while only one out of twenty knife attacks ends in death (Mikva 302). In addition, University of Wisconsin psychologist Leonard Berkowitz has found that guns can themselves stimulate aggressive behavior. According to Professor Berkowitz, "the finger pulls the trigger . . . but the trigger may also be pulling the finger" (qtd. in Mikva 300). Guns are more harmful than other weapons and without guns, many murders might not occur.

The counterargument, "even without a gun, a murder can still be committed," is refuted by quoting authorities, citing a fact, and citing statistics.

In the following example, the writer, who argues that Europe and Japan will not become the next superpowers, refutes the counterargument that the American economy has already declined. What techniques does the writer use to refute this counterargument?

> Finally, many believe that the American economy has already declined. At a superficial level, with Japanese products being sold all over the world, this may appear to be true. However, many American companies, such as GM, Ford, and IBM, have well-established and strong international markets (Pearson 41). Each year, *Fortune* magazine announces the world's 500 largest industrial companies. In 1990, the biggest company was GM, the third was Exxon, and the fourth largest company was Ford. IBM was number five, and remains fully three times the size of Japan's Fujitsu (number 63 in the *Fortune* list), which is the world's second largest computer maker. Six of the top ten and 164 of the top 500 companies are American, and only one of the top ten and 111 of the top 500 are Japanese (Hammes and Teitelbaum 244). The United States economy is obviously very strong.

When you are researching your paper and identifying counterarguments, you may find some counterarguments that are in fact valid or that you can only partially refute. When you find such counterarguments, you must be prepared to include them in your paper so that you will seem fair and objective.

RESEARCH PAPER FORMAT

Assignment 3 is written as a research paper, according to a clearly defined format. This section explains the format.

Paper: Use only white, 8 1/2-by-11-inch paper.

Margins: Leave one-inch margins on all four sides of the text.

Indentions: Indent the first line of a paragraph 5 spaces from the left margin, and bring all subsequent lines to the left margin. Indent all set-off (block) quotations 10 spaces from the left margin. Indentions within set-off quotations should be 13 spaces from the left margin.

Quotations: Run short quotations (fewer than five typed lines) into the text and enclose them in double quotation marks. Add the parenthetical citation that gives the source of the quotation, and then appropriate punctuation. For example:

According to Abner J. Mikva, the former Congressman from Illinois, "statistics show that a gun kept around the house is six times as likely to kill a family member as it is to kill an intruder" (300).

Block quotations do not require quotation marks.

Spacing: The research paper should be double-spaced throughout.

Here is a sample of the first page of a research paper:

```
                                                        Tan 1

    Teck-Ann Tan

    Dr. Braine

    EH 102

    12 August 1993

                Gun Control: A Fundamental Step to

            Reduce the Rate of Gun-Related Deaths and Crimes

            According to recent research, the American handgun

    homicide rate was 77 times that of countries which have

    strict gun control laws, such as . . .
```

Do not underline the title, or put it in quotation marks, or capitalize all the letters. Do not use a period after the title. Number all pages in the upper right-hand corner of the page. Type your last name before the page number. For example:

```
                                                        Tan 5

    increase in non-gun homicide" in Boston (120). According to

    the Federal Bureau of Investigation (FBI), almost two-thirds

    of all killings in 1973 resulted from arguments between

    friends or among family members. Most of these killings

    might
```

Works Cited: Always start the Works Cited on a new page. Type Works
Cited one inch from the top, centered between margins. Do not
punctuate. All entries should be double-spaced. Begin each entry on
the left margin and indent succeeding lines in each entry five
spaces. Periods mark ends of sections for author, title, and facts of
publication. Two spaces follow each period or colon; one space follows a comma. The entries should be alphabetized. Chapter 8 contains many examples of Works Cited sections.

```
                                                   Bavikati 10

                          Works Cited

Akamatsu, Paul. Japan-History-Restoration, 1853-1870. New

     York: Harper & Row, 1972.
```

Here is a sample page from a research paper:

```
                                               Tan 5

paragraph   and, while the African population has grown at a rate of

            3.2 percent annually, agricultural production has only grown

            at 1.1 percent (Jaycox 16).

new              However, Lathardus Goggins, Professor of African
paragraph   Studies at the University of Akron, argues that

set-off              despite this gloomy picture, Africa can draw encour-
quotation        agement from Third World models, including its own.

                 India and China, for example, in the face of griev-

                 ous economic obstacles, succeeded in growing enough

                 food to supply populations greater than all of Af-

                 rica. Botswana launched a famine relief program that

                 worked. Zimbabwe, aided by rain and strong leader-

                 ship, reversed its food production decline. (37)

new              In addition, a fairer treatment of African products in
paragraph   the world market would produce incentives for the farming

            communities of Africa. The farmers would be induced to pro-

            duce more for export, causing an increase . . .
```

ASSIGNMENT 3: WRITING TO PERSUADE

In Assignment 1, you expressed your knowledge and opinions on the research topic you had selected. In Assignment 2, you laid the foundation for the research process by informing your classmates of some of the important information contained in sources relevant to your topic. In Assignment 3, you will take a position and argue in support of your topic. Your aim is to persuade your readers to take your position seriously.

Your third writing assignment is an argumentative research paper. This paper will reflect all the writing skills you have acquired thus far, with emphasis on the methods of argument presented in this chapter.

You may also use methods of development discussed in earlier chapters, such as definition, illustration, and classification.

In Assignment 2, you combined information from two or more sources cited in your working bibliography. Your purpose was to inform your classmates about your research paper topic.

For Assignment 3, the persuasive paper, use at least six sources from your working bibliography (including, if you choose, the sources used in Assignment 2) to write a paper taking a position on your topic. Your aim is to persuade your readers to accept your position or at least to take it seriously.

Your thesis statement should guide you in the selection of relevant material from your sources. Remember to make a claim clearly and arguably; support the claim with facts, statistics, and quotations from authorities; anticipate counterarguments; and use a reasonable tone.

Turn in all notes, bibliographies, and drafts you use in writing the paper. If necessary, this supporting material should enable your instructor to reconstruct the process by which your paper was produced. If your supporting material proves inadequate, the grade on your paper may be lowered substantially.

Whenever you quote, paraphrase, or summarize from a source, remember to cite the reference within the text. When you quote directly, a photocopy of the page(s) from which you quoted, with the relevant section(s) highlighted, should be included in the supporting material you turn in with your paper. Limit the amount of direct quotation to about 10 to 15 percent of your paper's total length.

Use the MLA format and documentation style. *The MLA Handbook for Writers of Research Papers* (Fourth Edition) is the best reference. (Most libraries have several reference copies.)

Your paper should be a minimum of 1250 words or five to six double-spaced typed or computer-written pages. The length does not include the Works Cited page. Your instructor will tell you when your first draft and final version are due.

Please adhere strictly to all of these guidelines.

PROGRESS REPORT

Assignment 3, since it includes information from the previous assignments and follows a specific format, is the longest and most complex assignment in this course. Therefore, you will be asked to submit a progress report to your instructor so that he or she may know how you are handling the research and the writing required for the assignment. You can use the accompanying form for this report.

PROGRESS REPORT

Name _____   Date _____

Research topic _____

Please give me the following information on your Assignment 3. Be as concise as possible, but give me enough information so that I know how you are doing. Write on the back if necessary.

1. What have you accomplished so far?

2. What work do you still have to do? What is your schedule for finishing?

3. Have you had any problems with your paper that you haven't been able to solve? If you are still having problems, what are your plans for solving them?

4. Is there anything else you would like to tell me about your paper?

READINGS

To help you write Assignment 3, we have included two papers written by students. As you read these papers, note how the writers have used thesis statements to express their ideas and how they have used different methods, such as examples, description and narration, definition, classification, comparison and contrast, and argumentation, to develop their ideas. You will see that the writers have used tables and figures in their papers. Also, note how they have used and acknowledged sources through the use of paraphrase, summary, and quotation. The study questions at the end of each paper will guide you in group discussions.

For more examples of student papers, refer to Chapter 5, "Developing a Portfolio," and the additional readings.

Teck-Ann Tan

Dr. Braine

EH 102

12 August 1993

Gun Control: A Fundamental Step

to Reduce the Rate of Gun-Related

Deaths and Crimes

According to recent research, the American handgun homicide rate was 77 times that of countries which have strict gun-control laws, such as England, Japan, Sweden, and Canada (Robertson 202). However, the United States is still importing, manufacturing, and selling millions of guns each year, which has caused the rate of gun-related crimes to increase rapidly. The United States needs to have strict gun-control laws now, because guns have become the major cause of deaths and violent crimes in the country. Although strict gun-control laws cannot stop crimes and deaths, they may reduce the rate.

The first reason why the United States should have strict gun-control laws is because the laws may reduce the number of deaths caused by accidental shootings. Figure 1 on page 2 shows the deaths from firearm accidents from 1962 to 1967.

As Figure 1 shows, the number of accidental deaths from firearms in 1962 was 1,970. However, by 1967, the number had increased to 2,900. From 1962 to 1967, the annual average number of accidental deaths due to firearms was 2,378, of which 31 percent were children under fifteen years of age

Tan 2

(*Firearms and Violence* 26). Accidents occur because most gun-owning households keep their guns loaded and do not keep them locked away. Tragedy occurs when a child takes a gun and plays with it like a toy. For instance, in 1987, "six young boys were shot playing cops and robbers with their parents' or their relatives' guns in a suburb of Houston" ("Have Gun" 23). These tragedies will happen again as long as there are guns in houses. This is because children are curious about everything and will play with anything, including a gun, although they have been told that guns are dangerous. Innocent lives can be saved only if strict gun-control laws are enforced.

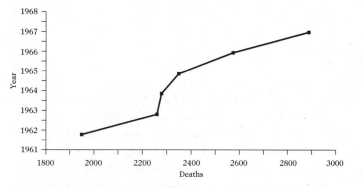

Fig. 1 Accidental Deaths from Firearms, 1962-1967. *Firearms and Violence in American Life: A Staff Report Submitted to the National Commission on the Causes and Prevention of Violence.* George D. Newton, Jr., Director, and Franklin E. Zimring, Director of Research. (Washington: GPO, no date.)

Secondly, the United States should have strict gun-control laws because the American handgun homicide rate is too high. Table 1 presents the number of murders and the types of weapons used from 1984 to 1988.

Table 1

Number of Murders in the United States and the Types of Weapons Used (1984-1988)

Year	Handgun	Cutting Instrument	Other	Total Murders
1984	59%	21%	20%	16,689
1985	59	21	20	17,545
1986	59	20	21	19,257
1987	59	20	21	17,895
1988	61	19	20	18,269

Source: United States Dept. of Justice. *Sourcebook of Criminal Justice.* (Washington: GPO, 1990.)

These statistics clearly show that handguns are the major weapons used in murders. In 1988, of the 18,269 murders committed in the United States, 10,296, or 61 percent, were committed with handguns. In Canada, a country which has strict gun-control laws, only 27 percent of all murders were gun related (Kleinman 3293). This shows that guns make killing easier. In addition, Philip J. Cook, Professor of Public Policy Studies and Economics at Duke University, has pointed out that the seriousness of robbery

and assault incidents is influenced by weapon type. A reduction in gun availability would cause some weapon substitution and probably little change in overall robbery and
assault rates--but the homicide rate would be reduced (63).

The third reason why the United States should have
strict gun-control laws is because it might reduce the rate
of aggravated assaults. Table 2 presents the number of
aggravated assaults and the types of weapons used from 1984
to 1988.

Table 2

Number of Aggravated Assaults and the Types of Weapons Used
(1984-1988)

Year	Handgun	Cutting Instrument	Other	Total
1984	21%	23%	56%	594,440
1985	21	23	56	663,891
1986	21	22	57	794,573
1987	21	21	58	792,987
1988	21	20	60	784,053

Source: United States Dept. of Justice. *Sourcebook of
Criminal Justice.* (Washington: GPO, 1990.)

According to Table 2, the percentage of aggravated
assaults from 1984 to 1988 remained at 21 percent. However,
during the same period, the total number of aggravated
assaults had increased from 594,440 to 784,053, which

suggests that the actual number of gun-related assaults
might have increased by nearly 39,000 cases. This number is
likely to keep on increasing if the government allows
criminals to obtain guns easily.

Finally, with strict gun-control laws, the U.S.
government should be able to reduce the number of robberies.
Table 3 presents the number of robberies in the United
States and the types of weapons used from 1984 to 1988.

Table 3

Number of Robberies and Types of Weapons Used (1984-1988)

Year	Handgun	Cutting Instrument	Other	Total
1984	36%	13%	51%	435,732
1985	35	13	52	461,725
1986	34	14	52	531,468
1987	33	14	53	498,632
1988	33	14	53	485,522

Source: United States Dept. of Justice. *Sourcebook of
    Criminal Justice.* (Washington: GPO, 1990.)

As shown in Table 3, in 1988, the number of gun-related
robberies in the United States was 485,522, or 33 percent of
the total number of robberies. Although the percentage was 2
percent less when compared with 1984, guns were still the most
commonly used weapon in robberies. Many robberies would not
succeed if criminals did not have a powerful weapon like a gun.

Tan 6

When discussing gun control, those who oppose such
actions will cite a number of reasons for opposing gun
control. First, they say that even without a gun, a murder
can still be committed. However, this may not be the case.
According to Glen L. Pierce, Director of the Center for
Applied Research at Northeastern University, the Bartetley-
Fox gun law "reduced gun homicide with no increase in non-
gun homicide" in Boston (120). According to the Federal
Bureau of Investigation (FBI), almost two-thirds of all
killings in 1973 resulted from arguments between friends or
among family members. Most of these killings might have
ended with nothing more than a fistfight if there had been
no gun in the house. Furthermore, one out of five gun
attacks ends in death, while only one out of twenty knife
attacks ends in death (Mikva 302). In addition, University
of Wisconsin psychologist Leonard Berkowitz has found that
guns can themselves stimulate aggressive behavior. According
to Professor Berkowitz, "the finger pulls the trigger . . .
but the trigger may also be pulling the finger" (qtd. in
Mikva 300). Guns are more harmful than other weapons and
without guns, many murders might not occur.

The second most common argument made by gun proponents
is that they need guns to protect themselves against
intruders. However, according to Abner J. Mikva, the former
Congressman from Illinois, "statistics show that a gun
kept around the house is six times as likely to kill a
family member as it is to kill an intruder" (300). In
addition, according to the National Committee on Violence,

in one year, more gun owners were killed in gun accidents
than were killed by robbers and burglars in the four
preceding years combined (Mikva 302). Keeping a handgun in
the house is apparently a dangerous practice.

Finally, the favorite argument of gun-control opponents
is the Second Amendment to the Constitution, which gives
Americans the right to bear arms. However, at least on four
occasions, the Supreme Court has held that this right is
limited to state militias and does not extend to private
citizens (Mikva 300). Every right has its limits, and rights
guaranteed by the Second Amendment should not be exploited
by those who use this argument to oppose gun control.

Walter E. Fauntroy, a former Congressman from the
District of Columbia, said, "I am tired of gun funerals"
(306). In fact, most Americans are tired of gun-related
crimes and deaths. According to one survey, 71 percent of
American citizens want handguns to be banned (U.S. Dept. of
Justice 174). James Blose, a researcher specializing in
criminal justice programs, explained that the major reason
why America still does not have strict gun-control laws is
because "in the federal arena, anti-gun control forces have
been supremely effective in blocking the majority's demand
for more stringent regulation of firearms" (81). Guns are
more harmful than drugs because they can kill people faster
than drugs do. If drugs are prohibited in America, there is
no reason why guns should be allowed. In order to have a
safe place to live, Americans should work harder to overcome
the anti-gun control forces, and push for strict gun-control
laws.

Tan 8

Works Cited

Blose, James. "State Programs for Screening Handgun Buyers."
     *Annals of the American Academy of Political and Social
     Science* 455 (1981): 80-91.

Cook, Philip J. "The Effect of Gun Availability on Violent
     Crime Patterns." *Annals of the American Academy of
     Political and Social Science* 455 (1981): 63-79.

Fauntroy, Walter E. "Should Manufacture and Sale of Handguns
     for Private Use Be Prohibited in the United States?"
     Congressional Digest Dec. 1990: 304-308.

*Firearms and Violence in American Life: A Staff Report
     Submitted to the National Commission on the Causes and
     Prevention of Violence.* George D. Newton, Jr.,
     Director, and Franklin E. Zimring, Director of
     Research. Washington: GPO, no date.

"Have Gun, Will Shoot." *The Economist* 23 Jan. 1988: 23.

Kleinman, Joel C. "International and Interstate Comparisons
     of Homicide Among Young Males." *Journal of the American
     Medical Association* 7 Nov. 1990: 3292-95.

Mikva, Abner J. "Should Manufacture and Sale of Handguns for
     Private Use Be Prohibited in the United States?"
     Congressional Digest Dec. 1990: 300-303.

Pierce, Glenn L., and William J. Bowers. "The Bartetley-Fox
     Gun Law's Short-Term Impact on Crime in Boston." *Annals
     of the American Academy of Political and Social Science*
     455 (1981): 120-37.

Robertson, Ian. *Sociology.* New York: Wort, 1988.

United States Dept. of Justice. *Sourcebook of Criminal
     Justice.* Washington: GPO, 1990.

Study Questions for Teck-Ann Tan's Paper

1. What is the thesis statement of this paper?

2. Does the thesis statement contain an issue that can be argued? (Yes or no).

3. Does the thesis statement contain a qualifier? (Yes or no).

4. Does each paragraph contain a topic sentence? (Yes or no).

5. What arguments does Tan use to support the thesis? (Look for the main arguments that he uses, as well as quotations, facts, and statistics.)

6. What counterarguments does Tan include in the paper?

7. How are the counterarguments refuted?

8. Specify places in the paper where more support is needed.

9. What methods of development does Tan use, other than argumentation? Look for examples, definitions, descriptions, narration, classification, and comparison and contrast.

10. What are the strengths of this paper?

11. How could this paper be improved? Note especially questions you wish Tan had answered or places where he needs to provide more support.

12. Has Tan documented his sources properly?

Espinoza 1

Nelvy Espinoza

Dr. Braine

EH 102

2 December 1993

African Famines: Can the Victims Be Saved?

According to recent statistics, Africa has the highest rate of infant mortality in the world, totaling more than 150 deaths per 1,000 live births. What is killing these infants? The answer is hunger. Africa is now experiencing the worst famine since 1972, when the first modern-day famine appeared in the Sahel and Ethiopia. This year, African famine victims are estimated to be 25 million, ten times the number of Kurds displaced by the Gulf War (Breslau 46). However, while the Kurds received much publicity, the African famine is no longer news. Although a solution to the famine appears to be impossible anytime soon, what may be possible is a reduction of the number of victims through a series of actions. These actions are the development of agriculture in Africa, a fairer treatment of African products in the world market, and a better utilization of African resources.

Africa possesses an area of about 30.3 million square kilometers of arable land and a population which is 70 percent agrarian. Therefore, the development of the agricultural sector in Africa could accelerate the annual increase in food production from 1.1 to 3 or 4 percent, achieving self-sufficiency in food (Okigbo 13). Africa is not feeding itself although it has the potential resources to produce more food than its population requires.

Espinoza 2

Developing African agriculture means an efficient management of agricultural and natural resources through an adequate knowledge of the African environment. This may require the adoption of a series of measures such as the communal use of modern machines, services, and fertilizer. Also, new techniques of cultivation such as crop rotation and intensive farming using the oases of deserts could be adopted ("Africa: Environmental" 259). For these measures and techniques to be adopted, the direct participation of African governments and international assistance is extremely important.

The International Agricultural Research Center (IARC), an institution which conducts research and training programs, is giving assistance to some African communities. IARC is training farmers in agricultural production, distribution, and training systems, and also teaching the farmers to focus on crops that will give them a competitive edge in the world market (Okigbo 14). Government intervention is necessary to provide the subsidies needed to acquire proper irrigation systems, farm equipment, storage facilities, and the construction of rural roads.

Some economists argue that all of these measures taken to develop African agriculture will greatly increase government expenditure; however, this increase can be offset by foreign aid and lending through the World Bank. In addition, if these programs are fully implemented, Africa's food and agricultural crisis could be solved by the year 2000 (Jaycox 18).

Espinoza 3

Others argue that the majority of African countries are still unable to produce enough food to meet even the minimum requirements of their expanding population. While the population of Africa has grown at the rate of 3.2 percent, the agricultural production has increased only at the rate of 1.1 percent (Jaycox 16). However, Lathardus Goggins, Professor of African Studies at the University of Akron, argues that

> despite this gloomy picture, Africa can draw
> encouragement from Third World models, including
> its own. India and China, for example, in the
> face of grievous economic obstacles, succeeded in
> growing enough food to supply populations greater
> than that of all Africa. Botswana launched a fam-
> ine relief program that worked. Zimbabwe, aided
> by rain and strong leadership, reversed its food
> production decline. ("Africa: Environmental" 259)

In addition, a fairer treatment of African products in the world market would produce incentives for the farmers of Africa. The farmers would be induced to produce more for export, causing an increase in government revenue, which in turn could be used in subsidies for communities most affected by the famine. Better prices would also encourage self-sufficiency. Farmers in Zimbabwe, Tanzania, and Zambia have already proven that they can feed their own countries if they get adequate prices (Ignatieff 17). The open market and free trade promoted by the International Monetary Fund and the World Bank were created to generate equal benefits and opportunities for all participants, but high taxes have

decreased the demand for African products in the world
market. For instance, the 8 percent tax imposed in 1980 for
cotton caused cotton exports to decrease by 8.6 percent
(Tages 15). Such actions hamper the plans of African
governments, because the funds to finance economic
development plans depend to a large extent on income from
agricultural exports. Table 1 shows how world market prices
have affected the export of five African agricultural
products.

Table 1

Impact of World Market Prices on African Agricultural
Products

Product	1989 Price	Export Rate	1990 Price	Export Rate
Sugarcane	.475	65.7%	.455	59.8%
Bananas	.330	64.0%	.383	67.6%
Oranges	.737	70.4%	.776	72.3%
Peanuts	.215	16.5%	.197	10.4%
Cotton	.835	73.8%	.818	65.2%

Source: *The Europe World Year Book,* 1991, Vol. II.

   As Table 1 shows, it is clear that some products had
better prices in 1989 than in 1990. Therefore, 1989 export
rates were better than for 1990. The statistics also
indicate that a reduction of prices has a greater impact on
African agricultural products than an increase in prices.
For example, in 1990, the price for bananas increased from
.330 to .383, causing a 3.6 percent increase in exports.

Espinoza 5

However, when the price of cotton dropped from .835 to .818, the exports fell by 8.6 percent (Collins 39). In fact, the drop in prices of major African export products caused a loss greater than the total foreign aid that Africa receives. A fairer treatment of African products in the world market is needed because African economic growth is closely related to their earnings from exports.

Finally, the number of victims of African famine may be reduced by a more efficient use of the overflowing resources of industrialized countries. While 25 million Africans starve, many industrialized countries face food surpluses (Jaycox 15). In the United States, grain is used to feed livestock and pumpkins are used to make funny faces during Halloween. According to environmentalist John Robbins, author of *Diet for a New America,* the grains and soybeans used to feed American livestock in one year could feed over a billion people. About sixteen pounds of grains, enough for eight African families for a day, are needed to produce a pound of beef, consumed by two people in America (qtd. in Langdon 4). In other developed countries, apples are fed to pigs. As Richard Atkinson points out in *Nutrition Reviews,* the number of apples used to feed a pig in one month could nourish over twenty Africans (qtd. in Langdon 4). A change in the way industrialized countries use their resources could enable them to share their overflowing tables with the victims of famine.

Even though the famine in Africa appears to be uncontrollable, I believe there is hope for the Africans. Although approximately twenty-five million people are

victims of the African famine, a 10 percent reduction in
American meat consumption alone could save sixty million
people. By developing agriculture in Africa, paying fairer
prices to African products in the world market, and
encouraging more efficient use of the resources of
industrialized countries, many victims of famine could
benefit. Although the implementation of all these plans will
take time, and perhaps they may not be beneficial to
everyone, millions of lives could be saved.

Espinoza 7

Works Cited

"Africa: Environmental Concerns." *The Encyclopedia
     Americana*. 1990 ed.

Breslau, Karen. "Sudan: The Silent Dying." *Newsweek* 15 April
     1991: 46.

Collins, Askin. "What About Africa?" *The Progressive* June
     1991: 39.

Ignatieff, Michael. "The Four Horsemen Are Here to Stay."
     World Press Review July 1991: 16-17.

Jaycox, Edward. "Ending Hunger in Africa." *Africa Report*
     Sept.-Oct. 1988: 15-18.

Langdon, Jim. "Did You Know?" *The Harbinger* 4-17 Nov. 1991:
     4.

Okigbo, Bede. "Finding Solutions to the Food Crisis." *Africa
     Report* Sept.-Oct. 1988: 13-14.

Robbins, John. *Diet for a New America*. Boston: Stillpoint,
     1990.

Tages, Abegier. "Helping Africa End Its Famine." *World Press
     Review* July 1991: 14-16.

Study Questions for Nelvy Espinoza's Paper

1. What is the thesis statement of this paper?

2. Does the thesis statement contain an issue that can be argued? (Yes or no).

3. Does the thesis statement contain a qualifier? (Yes or no).

4. Does each paragraph contain a topic sentence? (Yes or no).

5. What arguments does the writer use to support the thesis? (Look for the main arguments that the writer uses, as well as quotations, facts, and statistics.)

6. What counterarguments does Espinoza include in the paper?

7. How are the counterarguments refuted?

8. Specify places in the paper where more support is needed.

9. What methods of development does Espinoza use, other than argumentation? Look for examples, definitions, descriptions, narration, classification, and comparison and contrast.

10. What are the strengths of this paper?

11. How could this paper be improved? Note especially questions you wish Espinoza had answered or places where she needs to provide more support.

12. Has Espinoza documented her sources properly?

PLANNING/SELF-EVALUATION OF DRAFT

As in Chapters 6 and 8, we have included a Planning/Self-Evaluation of Draft form in order to help you with your paper. When you complete this form, you will have to think carefully about your paper. The form can also be used to self-evaluate your draft before your classmates peer-review it. Items 11 to 15 are mainly for your self-evaluation.

PLANNING/SELF-EVALUATION OF DRAFT

1. Tentative title:

2. My purpose in this paper is to argue that . . .

3. My thesis statement is . . .

4. My thesis contains the following issue:

5. My paragraphs will deal with the following topics:

   Paragraph 1:

   Paragraph 2:

   Paragraph 3:

   Paragraph 4:

   Paragraph 5:

   (Write the topics of other paragraphs on the back of this sheet.)

6. I have arranged the paragraphs in this order because . . .

7. I have used the following arguments in the paper:

   Argument 1:

   Argument 2:

   Argument 3:

   (Write additional arguments on the back of this sheet.)

8. I have used the following counterarguments:

   Counterargument 1:

   Counterargument 2:

   Counterargument 3:

   Counterargument 4:

   (Write additional counterarguments on the back of this sheet.)

(continued)

(continued)

9. I have used the following refutations:

Refutation 1:

Refutation 2:

Refutation 3:

Refutation 4:

(Write additional refutations on the back of this sheet. Remember, you may not have refutations for every counterargument.)

10. I have quoted the following authorities:

1.

2.

3.

4.

11. I need to define the following terms:

12. I need to develop the following points/paragraphs:

13. I need to omit the following sections because . . .

14. My opening is effective because . . .

15. My closing is effective because . . .

PEER REVIEW

In Chapters 6 and 8, you peer-reviewed papers your classmates wrote. We have provided a peer-review sheet for Assignment 3. As in the previous peer reviews, write your comments and suggestions after reading your class-mate's paper two or three times. Always offer specific comments and suggestions.

You may write comments directly on the writer's paper.

When you have completed writing comments and suggestions, go to the student whose paper you reviewed and further explain your comments and suggestions to him or her. Use the peer-review sheet to guide you in this discussion. As in previous peer reviews, remember to ask the writer questions.

ASSIGNMENT 3—PEER REVIEW

Author:

Reviewed by:

First, read the paper straight through to get a quick, general impression. On the second or third reading, respond to the paper according to the guidelines given below. Please offer specific comments and suggestions. After writing your responses, discuss the paper with the writer. Thank you.

1. Does the thesis statement contain an issue? (Yes or no).

2. Is the issue qualified? (Yes or no).

3. List evidence (quotations, facts, statistics) that support the issue.
    (a) First example:

    (b) Second example:

4. Did you find any counterarguments? (Yes or no).

If you answered yes to item 4, answer items 5, 6, and 7. If you answered no, go on to item 8.

5. List two counterarguments from the paper.
    (a)

    (b)

6. Is counterargument (a) refuted? (Yes or no).

7. Is counterargument (b) refuted? (Yes or no).

8. Is the introduction effective? (Yes or no).
    If not, can you suggest a more effective introduction?

9. Is the conclusion effective? (Yes or no).
   If not, can you suggest a better conclusion?

10. Is the paper well organized? (Yes or no).
    If not, indicate where the organization is not maintained.

11. Write the terms that need definitions.

12. Check for errors in spelling, grammar, and punctuation.

13. What are the strong points of this paper? Consider the questions you've used above to analyze the paper, as well as other criteria of good writing.

14. How can the paper be improved?

CHAPTER 10

Answering Essay Examinations

In order to get full credit for an essay examination, you should write a complete, well-organized, and well-written answer. When your answer is well organized and well written, it is easy to read and the instructor will be able to identify your main ideas quickly.

Of course, writing a good essay answer depends on your having something to say. This chapter thus begins with a discussion of how you can prepare to take an essay exam.

PREPARING FOR AN ESSAY EXAM: THE LONG VIEW

The best way to ensure that you do well in a course, including good scores on examinations, is to develop good study habits throughout the course. Especially important are regular attendance and adequate preparation.

You should realize by now that you need to attend class *every time* it meets, and you should be on time to every class as well. Regular, timely attendance conveys to your instructor that you are serious about the course and motivated to do well in it.

In addition to attending class regularly, you should listen carefully and take notes of important points during lectures. These notes will help you to review the important points when you study for exams.

Careful, thorough preparation for each class is also important preparation for the exams that come later in the course. For each class, read the assignment (an assigned chapter or a section of a book, for example) thoughtfully, underlining or highlighting important ideas and examples. You will want to review them later when you study for exams. In fact, it's a good idea to read each assignment more than once. Some students also find it helpful to make outlines of assigned reading materials, which they can then review just before class and again as they are studying for exams.

If you are having any trouble in understanding the course material, you can get additional help in several ways. You might form a study group with other members of the class to review assignments and class notes. Your instructor probably will be available to you during office hours to explain specific areas where you are having trouble. If you go to your instructor for help, have specific questions in mind that you would like answered and keep the conference as brief as possible, since instructors have many students and responsibilities.

The best long-term strategy for doing well in a course, including getting good grades on essay exams, is regular, serious attendance in class and preparation of assigned materials. Cramming the night before an exam is *not* the best way to prepare!

PREPARING FOR AN ESSAY EXAM: CLOSE TO TEST TIME

Close to the time you will take an essay exam, perhaps a week in advance, you should begin a focused review of the material the exam will cover. If you have prepared thoroughly as the material has been assigned, this review should not be difficult.

The place to start your review is your lecture notes, any problems or exercises you have been assigned, and the assigned readings. Reread and restudy this material, focusing particularly on what you have underlined or highlighted. If you haven't already made outlines of notes and readings, now is the time to do so.

It may also be a good idea to form a study group to review for the exam. Members of the group can share outlines they have made and clarify any areas that may be confusing to some of the students in the group. It may be helpful for the group to brainstorm in order to predict the essay questions on the exam and then to prepare outlines of hypothetical answers.

Anticipating questions the instructor may ask on the exam is a good strategy to follow whether or not you study in a group. Often exam questions come from concepts the instructor has emphasized in class. Major ideas covered in the assigned readings are also likely topics for exam questions. As you prepare for the exam, look for possible questions the instructor might ask. Then outline answers you could write to those questions so that you'll be prepared to respond quickly if those questions appear on the exam. With any luck, at least some of the questions you have predicted will be on the exam.

TAKING THE EXAM

In essay exams, you will be asked to write about a topic in your own words. That is, you will be summarizing and paraphrasing without having access to the sources while writing the exam. This may create some anxiety in students who have not mastered English grammar and have a limited English vocabulary. But research shows that many instructors do not penalize for minor errors in grammar, spelling, and punctuation when they grade essay exams. Most instructors also do not count the number of facts that have been included in an answer. Instead, they look for ability to organize ideas properly and to support them with evidence. In short, they look for a well-organized and well-written answer.

You will see that an essay exam answer is similar to nonexamination writing assignments, such as those in this course. Both require you to organize your ideas and support them with evidence. However, the two writing situations have clear differences. In an essay exam, you will not be able to get the help of your classmates in peer reviews or to visit the writing lab. You will also have little or no time to revise or rewrite the paper. In effect, your answer is a first draft of a paper, which means that you will have to carefully review and edit the paper yourself.

The following strategies will help you be successful in taking essay exams.

1.   When you first receive the examination, read the entire exam carefully so that you can use your time wisely. If the instructor has given you a choice of questions, choose the question(s) you can answer best. If you don't have a choice, answer the easiest questions first.

2.   Read the instructions for the exam carefully. This way, you will not overlook something the instructor expects. For instance, if the instructor wants you to answer four questions and you answer three, you will lose 25 percent of the points. If, on the other hand, you answer four questions when the instructor wants only three, you will have wasted time. If you don't understand the instructions or some of the questions, politely ask the instructor for clarification. Once you have reviewed the entire exam and divided the time you have among the questions, you are ready to work on individual questions. To ensure that you have a well-written answer, it's helpful to follow several steps when answering each question. These steps are described in items 3 to 7 below.

3.   Read the question carefully, at least twice. Underline key words and phrases in the question to be sure that you understand what is being asked and what kind of answer the instructor expects to see. For example, if you just describe two theories when the instructor wants you to discuss their differences, you will lose valuable points. Box 10.1 lists some common key words used in essay exam questions. Study them carefully.

4.   Brainstorm the topic so that you write down every idea or example that might be related to the question. Write your ideas down as quickly as they come to you; don't stop to evaluate them or to arrange them in order.

5.   After you have finished brainstorming, reread the question to be sure you haven't missed something important. Then evaluate the ideas and examples you have written, eliminating those ideas that are not relevant to the question you are answering; you may also think of additional information to include in your answer. Arrange your ideas and examples into a rough outline, using arrows or numbers to sequence the ideas.

6.   Write your answer, keeping these guidelines in mind:

Begin your answer with a thesis statement that echoes the question and forecasts the main parts of your answer. The thesis statement will be the first paragraph of your essay; it may be from one to several sentences. Assume, for example, that you are asked the following question in an introductory English literature class:

BOX 10.1	*Some Key Words Used in Essay Exam Questions*
Key Word	*Meaning*
compare	Name the features of two things to show their similarities and differences.
contrast	Examine two things to emphasize their differences.
define	Give or explain the meaning of a term.
describe	Explain an item in greater detail. Draw a picture in words.
discuss	Examine in detail.
evaluate	Examine something according to its strengths and weaknesses, considering (pros) advantages and (cons) disadvantages.
explain	Make something clear and understandable.
identify	Name items that belong to a group or category.
illustrate	Give examples.
outline	Give the main ideas in a list.
prove	Show that something is true.
relate	Show the connection between two things.
summarize	Write the main points of a subject or topic.
support	Provide evidence to back up a point.

> Discuss the major periods of nineteenth-century English poetry. Identify the major characteristics of each period, and illustrate these characteristics by discussing several important authors and their writing.

To answer this question, you might begin with this thesis statement:

> Nineteenth-century English poetry is often divided into poetry of the Romantic and Victorian periods. Romantic poetry is characterized by an interest in nature, social reform, and the importance of individual experience. Victorian poetry may express these interests but also reflects anxiety over the changing nature of society and ideas.

You would then divide your essay into the two main parts suggested in your thesis. The first part would discuss Romantic poetry, and the second would cover the Victorian period.

Write in short paragraphs, each beginning with a strong topic sentence. Use topic sentences that echo the question and reflect the structure forecast in your thesis statement. Support your topic sentences with adequate details and examples. Depending on the length of your answer, you may need from one to several paragraphs for each main point of your essay. For instance, for your answer to the question on nineteenth-century English poetry, you might write a paragraph on each characteristic of Romantic poetry identified in your thesis: nature, social reform, and the importance of individual experience.

Use transitional words and phrases to guide the instructor through the answer.

7. After you've finished writing, reread your answer to check for grammatical and mechanical errors and to make sure that your sentences are clear and readable.

Even though you have limited time to prepare and write your answer, if you use these strategies, your chances of writing a good answer are improved. The key is to budget the time you have. Suppose you have 30 minutes to answer a question. You might then allow 5 minutes to plan your answer, 15 minutes to draft it, and 10 minutes to check and revise it.

Example:

Imagine that in a history class you have studied the history of Japan in the nineteenth and twentieth centuries. On an exam you might find the following question:

Discuss the changes that took place in Japan during the Meiji period.

When you brainstorm this topic, you realize that the Meiji period brought changes on social, political, and economic levels. You thus decide to organize your answer to the question into these three main sections.

You begin your answer with a thesis statement that summarizes the main idea of your answer and that echoes the question. This statement will be the first paragraph of your answer; in this case, it is a one-sentence paragraph:

Paragraph 1:

With the coming of the Meiji period, Japan began to be modernized on social, political, and economic levels.

You then begin the remaining three paragraphs of your answer with a topic sentence that helps the reader to identify the main idea discussed in that paragraph:

Paragraph 2:

On a social level, the Meiji government modified and later abolished the feudal class system. [Give details and examples to explain the social changes.]

Paragraph 3:

Major political changes also occurred during the Meiji period. [Add details and examples.]

Paragraph 4:

Finally, the economy of Japan also changed drastically during the Meiji period. [Add details and examples about the economic changes.]

Once you have drafted your answer, reread it carefully to be sure that you have expressed your ideas clearly and correctly. If you need to edit your answer, make changes as neatly as possible so that your answer will remain legible.

An Additional Suggestion

When you write your essay, write as legibly and neatly as possible and on every other line. Then, when you edit your answer, you can cross out and rewrite in the lines you have skipped, if necessary. But don't make your instructor struggle to read what you have written.

EXERCISE 10.1   ANSWERING ESSAY QUESTIONS

Assume the following questions appear on an exam in one of your courses. Answer the questions, using the strategies discussed in this chapter.

1. Discuss three differences between your native culture and the culture of the United States as you have experienced it as a student at this university.

2. What opportunities for business will your home country have in the next decade? What main problems must your country solve to take advantage of these opportunities?

3. How has your home country changed technologically in the past decade or so? What main changes do you foresee in the coming decade?

Additional Readings

THE WEAKER SEX?

Iheng-Si Ho

Throughout history women generally have had fewer legal rights and career opportunities than men. Wifehood and motherhood were regarded as women's most significant professions. In the 20th century, however, women in most countries have won the right to vote and have increased their educational and job opportunities. Perhaps most important, they have fought for and to a large degree won a reevaluation of traditional views of their role in society. Nevertheless, mankind still has conventional ideas of what women are or how they should behave in our modern civilization.

My father is an old-fashioned Chinese. He once said to my mother that raising a daughter was a waste of money and energy. Once she gets married, she would leave the family and change her last name to carry her husband's. It's like raising a child for someone else, he said. Being male and too young to understand how my sister would feel, I foolishly felt proud of what my father said and glanced at my sister with a superior attitude. Powerless, she looked at me with her tearful eyes. A deep sadness marked her face, a face that still haunts me after almost 15 years. We had never talked about it, but I hope she has no recollection of that incident. Today, thinking back, I'm as outraged as any decent human being would be. First because of my stupidity, and then because of my father's irresponsibility and his lack of respect toward women.

Maternity, the natural biological role of women, has traditionally been regarded as their major social role. The fact that people stereotype women as "housewife" has largely determined the ways in which women have expressed themselves. Today, legalized abortion has given them greater control over the number of children they will bear. Although such developments have freed women for roles other than motherhood, the social pressure for women to become wives and mothers still prevents many talented women from finishing college or pursuing careers.

Even though there is an increasing number of female doctors and lawyers around the world today, some fields such as engineering or computer science are still viewed as men's. I was on the Internet the other day chatting with a French engineering student at the university of Paris. A particular thing about the Internet is that you don't see who you are talking to, and neither does your conversational companion at his or her computer screen. We started to talk about computers and then went on to other subjects. During our conversation, I was told how freezing it was in Paris that day, especially if you are wearing a skirt. A skirt? I thought. I first took it as a joke, but then realized I had been communicating with a female. We had been talking for an hour or so, and the word "female" never crossed my mind. The term "engineer" led me to believe that it was a male. I did everything I could to not let her be aware of my surprise. And since she couldn't see the expression on my face, it was all much easier. We continued chatting as if nothing had happened.

In today's society, difference often means discrimination. And as long as there is inequality, there will be people out there fighting it. Even though numerous things have definitely changed in the past century, there are still too many examples of sex discrimination. If equality of both sexes exists, my essay would be irrelevant and I would have most probably chosen another topic.

THE LOSS OF HUMAN RIGHTS IN HONDURAS

Norman Martin Aviles

The past fourteen years have not been an easy period for Hondurans. The establishment of a left-wing government in Nicaragua in 1979 and the uprisings of guerrilla forces in El Salvador created a tense situation within Honduras. The military suspected the civilian population of subversion. As a result, "during the early 1980s, Honduras witnessed a dramatic erosion of respect for human rights" (*Honduras* 4). Illegal arrests, torture, extrajudicial executions, and disappearances are examples of the human rights violations that have been committed by the armed forces in Honduras.

Illegal arrests and torture have long been practiced by the military. In 1982, General Gustavo Alvarez Martinez, Commander-in-Chief of the armed forces, created and headed a secret service which is considered responsible for illegal arrests, torture and interrogation of people in secret jails (*Honduras* 10). Among the victims were many leaders of popular organizations such as union workers, students, teachers, and those suspected to have links with the Salvadorian-guerrillas. An ex-member of Honduras Army Intelligence, Florencia Caballero, described that victims were tortured with "as many electrical prods on their genitals as necessary . . . until they talked and all were killed" (LeMayne 7).

Information obtained by Amnesty International shows an alarming abuse of power by the army. In 1987, "Out of 54 detentions, only three apparently resulted in criminal prosecutions. [Often] there was not an arrest order. . . . Court officials also said that many detainees had no legal charges to face" (LeMayne 26). The Committee for the Defense of Human

Rights in Honduras (CODEH) revealed that in 1991, 55 homicides were committed by military members who were recognized; in 17 cases the murderers were not recognized, but military agents were under suspicion. In the same year, in 156 recorded cases of torture, 51 victims were tortured until they pleaded guilty; and 68 were tortured while they were in the Central Penitentiary. There were also 718 illegal detentions and the police committed 29 out of 30 housebreakings (*CODEH Bulletin* 7). In 1992, the situation was no better.

> [I]n 19 out of 25 homicides, military members were under suspicion. The army was responsible for 25 assaults against peoples, 42 attacks to private property, 82 cases of torture and maltreatment, 164 illegal detentions, 56 cases of failure to respect judicial procedures, 10 illegal housebreakings, 1 attempt against freedom of expression, 4 attempts against freedom of reunion, and 7 against freedom of movement. ("Shaking in the Barracks" 4–5)

Extrajudicial executions and disappearances are part of the violations committed by the army. According to the National Commissioner for Human Rights Protection, 179 cases of disappearances occurred in Honduras between 1980 and 1992 (*The Facts Speak* 69). According to the Commissioner, the kidnappings and executions were practiced by specialized groups within the armed forces such as the National Investigations Division (DNI), military intelligence or G-2, and particularly by the secret intelligence force known as Battalion 3-16. A striking example of a disappearance is presented by Claudio Grossman: "Manfredo Angel Valesquez Rodriquez was taken into the detention center in Tegucigalpa on September 12, 1981, and was never seen again. . . . Without any judicial process he was detained, interrogated and tortured, and then disappeared" (363). *The Facts Speak for Themselves* records another case of disappearance: Juan Alberto Sanchez was detained by the military in the presence of his parents on July 1, 1992, in the town of Santo Domingo in Colomoncagua. He has never been seen since that day (77).

In summary, the armed groups have committed many violations against human rights in Honduras. First, people have been executed and many others have died as a consequence of ill treatment during their detention; second, the detentions were followed by physical and psychological torture; and finally, many detainees were not given the right to a fair trial.

WORKS CITED

CODEH Bulletin. Committee for the Defense of Human Rights in Honduras. April–July 1992: 7.

Grossman, Claudio. "Disappearances in Honduras: The Need for Direct Victim Representation in Human Rights Litigation." *Hastings International and Comparative Law Review* 15 (1992): 363–89.

Honduras: Civilian Authority—Military Power: Human Rights Violations in the 1980s. New York: Amnesty International Publications, 1988.

LeMayne, James. "Honduras Army Linked to Death of 200 Civilians." *New York Times* 2 May 1987, late ed.: 1, 7, 26.

"Shaking in the Barracks." *La Presna* 21 Feb. 1993: 4–5.

The Facts Speak for Themselves. National Commissioner for Human Rights Protection. Tegucigalpa: Guaymuras, 1994.

THE STRUGGLE FOR AUTONOMY OF TWO ETHNIC GROUPS WITHIN RUSSIA: CRIMEAN TARTARS AND VOLGA GERMANS

Lyudmila S. Samsonova

The Socialist Revolution of 1917 considerably changed the life of many ethnic groups within Russia. It happened because the Communists believed in uniformity of human nature and did not recognize the meaning of blood relationships, nor could they accept the struggle of nations for self-expression. Moreover, according to Stalin's policies, Russians were the superior nation. As a consequence, the others, especially small ethnic groups, were treated as inferior and not reliable.

The implementation of such an idealogy resulted in mass deportations of Crimean Tartars and Volga Germans from their native lands to Siberia and Central Asia during World War II, for an alleged collaboration with fascist Germany (Conquest 211). In the 1990s, after the disintegration of the USSR, these two peoples are returning home and trying to reclaim the lands that belonged to them. Struggling for their rights and independence, Crimean Tartars and Volga Germans are both facing problems concerning rejection from the people now inhabiting their territories. I believe that a solution can be found if people will understand the complexity and the seriousness of these problems.

During the first years of the formation of the USSR, before Stalin came to power, some small nations within the Russian Soviet Federate Socialistic Republic (RSFSR) were given independence. Thus, on October 18, 1921, under Lenin's power, the Soviet Union established the Crimean Autonomous Soviet Socialistic Republic (Smith 325). Three years later, in 1924, the German Autonomous Volga Republic was formed (Moralis and Wildhagen 45). However, both republics were abolished after Stalin accused them of collaboration with invading German forces during World War II. More than 400,000 Germans of the Volga region (Conquest 212) and 250,000 Tartars of Crimea (Carney 40), were rounded up and dispersed to the "farthest and coldest" regions of the Soviet empire (Moralis and Wildhagen 45). During this deportation, more than 40% of the Tartars and 30% of the Germans died (Bremmer 24). Moreover, unlike deported residents of the Soviet Union's other republics, they were not permitted to return, nor were their republics restored even decades after the war (Conquest 41).

When Gorbachev came to power, the laws on the rehabilitation of people subjected to repression between 1941 and 1944 in the USSR were adopted. This gave rise to the national movements. For the governments, eventually, it became more important to preserve the rights of the people and ethnic communities than to preserve the illusion of a unified nation state (Smith 43). As a result, many Volga Germans and Crimean Tartars started to move back to their homelands. Today each ethnic group is asserting its right to self-determination and seeking to establish territorial borders for its people.

As people started moving back to their historical places, the first problem that arose was the potential conflict with the current inhabitants. The meetings on the streets of Simferopol and Saratov, the former capitals of the German and Crimean Republics, with demands to stop the invasion of aliens are the most common manifestations of this conflict (Gorelov 31). The main argument of those who try to prevent the flow of Volga Germans and Crimean Tartars to their homelands is that the regions they are coming back to never belonged to them.

To explain how so many Germans and Tartars found themselves within Russian borders one only needs to look back in history. It was Catherine the Great who added these ethnic groups to the already motley unit of nations within Russia. In a drive to develop the economy of Russia, she issued decrees inviting Germans from Prussia, Switzerland, and France to come and settle in the lands of the left bank of the Volga River, which were uninhabited at that time. In their article, "Home Sweet Volga," R. Moralis and A. Wildhagen state that "[b]y 1775 some 30,000 foreigners, mostly Germans, had settled along the Volga" (45). As a result of Catherine's policies, the Germans turned unproductive virgin land into fields and orchards. Furthermore, according to the Mustafa Dzhemilev, the leader of the movement of the Crimean Tartars, "Crimean Tartars are the only natives of Crimea" (Brumberg 63). Actually, Tartars had established their first state there already in the middle of the fifteenth century and controlled the peninsula until 1783, when the Turkish Khanate was defeated by Catherine the Great (Fisher 4, Carney 39).

The other reason for the opposition to the return of the Crimean Tartars and Volga Germans is the current populations' fear that German and Tartar will be established as national languages if autonomous republics are formed. This apprehension is understandable and natural. However, one has to admit that, when the USSR was formed, all non-Russian ethnic groups were forced to accept Russian as their first language instead of their own. Officially, the Germans and Tartars, who initially spoke their own languages, had to learn Russian from 1917 on. According to statistics of 1979, "Whereas almost half of non-Russian population [of the Republics] claimed a knowledge of Russian . . . only 3.5 percent of Russians could claim a similar knowledge of another Soviet language" (Smith 8). Moreover, when exiled to the Kazakhstan, Uzbekistan, and other Asian republics of the Soviet Union, they had to learn a third language up to a high level.

The experience of the Baltic republics proves that a solution to the language problem can be found. When Estonia, Latvia, and Lithuania separated from the Soviet Union in 1989, they offered an extensive network of free-of-charge services to help the Russian-speaking citizens, who constituted a third of the total population, in acquiring a new language (Smith 67). Many special courses were organized for those Russians who wished to stay and learn the language. A lot of books and study guides were published (Smith 69).

There is another reason for the conflict between Volga Germans and Russians living in the Volga region now. Because the German government is trying to help Volga Germans to establish their republic, the Russians are afraid of nationalism or Nazism. Some people are even talking about the restoration of "the Fourth Reich" (Gorelov 31). Many residents still remember the atrocities of the fascists. There was hardly a family that did not experience a loss of relatives. In addition, some of the people living in the Volga region were in concentration camps during the war, and it was not easy for them to believe that the formation of the German Republic would not bring them any harm. To prove their will to defend the rights of the Volga Germans and help them to get back to their historical homeland, German Chancellor Helmut Kohl agreed to allot 66 million dollars annually for development of the Volga region (Moralis and Wildhagen 45). He stressed that the German government is prepared to provide new roads, enterprises, cultural centers, and housing, not only for the German population of the future republic, but also for the Russian and Ukrainians living there ("Nationalities" 31).

In the case of the Crimean Tartars, the confrontation of local administrations and new settlers ended in violence. In 1989, there was the first incident of "organized violence against Tatars carried out by OMON, 'special forces'" (Bremmer 25). According to official data, 250,000 Crimean Tartars returned by 1992. Only 24,000 of 52,000 families have housing. Moreover, only 45 buildings out of 900 promised by the administration were opened (Semena 19). The Tartars began to build houses on land they could find. In June 1992, in Krasny Rai, the local authorities sent crowds of citizens with approximately 700 policemen to destroy the Crimean Tartars' tent city. However, it did not stop the Tartars from constructing apartments. Three months later, on the night of October 1, 120 state farmers and 600 policemen tore down all the houses. In the confrontation, 24 policemen and 26 Tartars were injured (Pilat 17). The Crimean prosecutor's office brought criminal charges against the victims of the attack themselves, the Crimean Tartars (Pilat 18).

To express their protest, between four and five thousand Tartars from every part of the peninsula gathered at the Crimean Supreme Soviet building. They demanded the release of all of those arrested during the events in Krasny Rai. The police attacked the demonstrators, and 30 Crimean Tartars were injured (Bremmer 25). The arrested Crimean Tartars were released, but this was not the end of the confrontation. M. Dzhemilev, the leader of the Crimean Tartars, had called for a general mobilization, and self-defense detachments were formed (Pilat and Skachko 29). I hope that in the near future the administrators will realize it is impossible to ignore the existence of 250,000 people, and that the problem of land will be solved. Otherwise, Crimean Tartars may declare themselves a people fighting for their national liberty, which can result in new bloodshed.

Unlike Crimean Tartars, who are literally fighting for their historical land which belonged to them for more than five centuries, the Volga Germans were allowed to form their own republic; however, certain conditions have been imposed. After his trip to the Volga region, Russian President Boris Yeltsin announced that autonomy is possible in only one case: if 90% of the population will be Germans ("On Volga" 15). The Germans cannot establish their republic because the local authorities cannot provide the Germans with places to live, jobs, German schools, or institutes. Moreover, it is impossible to increase the number of Germans up to 90% of the population (Gorelov 33). Therefore, the condition put forward by the Russian president actually deprived Germans of an opportunity to organize their autonomy on the Volga.

There are two choices for the Germans now. One is to move to Germany, and the second is to find some other place to form a republic. The first choice promises to be painful for those who leave and for those whom they leave. There are many Germans who cannot emigrate because they have Russian relatives; others have German blood but wish to stay in Russia ("Nationalities" 29). On the other hand, the Germans' departure will affect the economy of Russia. There are about 6 million Germans in Russia who, if they leave, will deprive the country of hard-working, disciplined people (Gorelov 32).

The second choice seems more acceptable to many Germans. Because the Germans were literally dispersed all over the country in 1941, they could form their republic on any available territory. Several territories have been suggested. The first choice made by Boris Yeltsin was a missile firing range. The Germans were given the opportunity to first clean up and cultivate this land full of artillery shells; the discussion of autonomy would come later ("On Volga" 16). According to Boris Petersm, the leader of the Russian Germans' society, many Germans considered this suggestion as an insult because "[t]he environmental characteristics of the former Soviet Union missile range do not even meet Soviet criteria for the permissible level of pollution" ("On Volga" 16).

Another proposed solution to the resettlement of Germans was within Kazakhstan, where about 333,000 Germans were removed during World War II (Wheeler 48). However, this idea was not approved by the indigenous population, provoking mass demonstrations among Kazakhs (Wheeler 50). As a result of Stalin's national policies, Kazakhstan was already overcrowded by the people of different nationalities, and did not want to lose its integrity and give a part of its land to the Germans.

The most popular decision on German resettlement was that concerning Tver Province, not far from Moscow, and Kaliningrad Province. First of all, the area of the Tver Province is unpopulated. There are only 1.5

people per one hundred hectares of the agricultural land. In addition, the settlements of the Germans in that area would provide Moscow with good crops ("Nationalities" 29). The other settlement available for the future German republic is the Kaliningrad region, which is the only place in Russia where there is not an indigenous population. This should prevent ethnic conflicts ("Nationalities" 30). Therefore, the territory for the German Autonomous Republic can be found within the Russian borders.

The overall indefinite position of the Crimean Tartars and Volga Germans is complicated by the political inconsistency of the Russian and local authorities. Boris Yeltsin, in his speech to the Volga Germans in January 1992, emphasized that "historical justice must be done with respect to a people illegally subjected to repression," ("On Volga" 15). However, not much work in this direction has been done by his government since then. The question of autonomy for the Tartars and Germans is not an easy one because one must consider all sides of the problem and the possible reasons for confrontation. The prejudices, fear of changes, and lack of sympathy and understanding are only some of them. The complexity of the issue does not mean that it is insoluble; it only means that one has to look for more opportunities and put more effort on the settling of problems.

WORKS CITED

Bremmer, Tan. "Ethnic Issues in Crimea." *RFE/RL Research Report* 30 April 1993: 24–29.

Brumberg, Abraham. "Whose Crimea?" *New York Review of Books* 22 Oct/ 1992: 63–64.

Carney, James. "Ready to Cast Off." *Time* 15 June 1992: 39–40.

Conquest, Robert. *Stalin: Breaker of Nations*. New York: Penguin Books, 1991.

Fisher, Alan. *The Crimean Tartars*. Bloomington: Hoover Institutional Press, 1978.

Gorelov, I. "Russia Without Russian Germans?" *Current Digest of the Post-Soviet Press* 5 Feb. 1992: 31–32.

Moralis, Richard, and Andreas Wildhagen. "Home Sweet Volga." *Forbes* 3 Feb. 1992: 45–46.

"Nationalities." *Current Digest of the Post-Soviet Press* 26 Feb. 1992: 29–31.

"On Volga Trip, Yeltsin Rebuffs Germans." *Current Digest of the Post-Soviet Press* 12 Feb. 1992: 15–18.

Pilat, Alexander. "The Situation Is Strained to the Limit." *Current Digest of the Post-Soviet Press* 4 Nov. 1992: 17–20.

Pilat, Alexander, and Vladimir Skachko. "Crimean Supreme Soviet Deems Activity of the Crimea Tartar People Unconstitutional." *Current Digest of the Post-Soviet Press* 11 Nov. 1992: 28–39.

Semena, Nikolai. "Crimean Tartars Seek Statehood." *Current Digest of the Post-Soviet Press* 1 Sept. 1993: 19–20.

Smith, Graham. *Nationalities Policy from Lenin to Gorbachev*. New York: Longman and London, 1992.

Wheeler, Geoffrey. *The Modern History of Soviet Central Asia*. New York: Prager, 1964.

INDEX